Robt E. Robinson

May 1862

Wm B. Frisby.

Oct. 1886.

AN

EXPOSITION

OF THE

EPISTLE OF SAINT PAUL TO THE ROMANS,

ACCORDING TO THE ANALOGY OF

THE CATHOLIC FAITH.

BY

THE REV. MORGAN DIX, A. M.

"Exstiterunt enim plures, qui cœlestium verborum simplicitatem pro voluntatis suæ sensu, non pro veritatis ipsius absolutione susciperent, aliter interpretantes quam dictorum virtus postularet. De intelligentia enim hæresis, non de Scriptura est: et sensus, non sermo fit crimen."—S. HILARY, DE TRINITATE.

NEW YORK:
PUBLISHED FOR THE AUTHOR,
AND FOR SALE AT 762 BROADWAY.
1863.

C. A. ALVORD, STEREOTYPER AND PRINTER.

TO

THE REV. JOHN McVICKAR, S. T. D.;

MOST GRATEFULLY REMEMBERED,

AS HAVING FIRST GUIDED ME IN THE STUDY OF PHILOSOPHY,

AND THEN DIRECTED ME TOWARD THAT SUBLIMER PURSUIT,

WHEREOF SHE IS THE HAND-MAID.

THE SCIENCE OF THEOLOGY;

THIS COMMENTARY IS, BY PERMISSION, INSCRIBED,

WITH THE RESPECT AND AFFECTION OF

ONE OF HIS OLD PUPILS.

PREFACE.

It may occasion surprise, that a parish priest, who, for the pressure of the daily and incessant duties of his office, has no time left for study, and scarce any for reflection, should yet have taken in hand to prepare a commentary upon a writing so hard to understand and explain as the Epistle to the Romans: and it may seem yet more strange that he should have the boldness to submit it to public inspection. But some excuse may be found in the object had in view. For this does not profess to be a critical or learned work; and it was not written for scholars. It is but an expression of the thoughts which a man may carry about with him as a part of his burden; which sometimes burn within him; and which he would impart to others as if for his own relief. And again, it is the result of the effort to make for himself what he wanted, and what no one else has given him thus far. Whosoever will study the word of God must, sooner or later, come to this Epistle; and whosoever comes to it must feel how very hard it is to comprehend; and the writer has not, in the course of his own reading, found any commentary on it which met those difficulties precisely as they have presented themselves to his mind, and which, at the same time, has aimed at harmonizing the words of the Apostle with the Creeds and System of the Catholic Church.

The chief impediments in the way of a right understanding of this Epistle are not found in the sacred text. They block the path while yet we approach. There are certain popular explanations of its meaning, which have not only attained to notoriety, but are thoughtlessly accepted, of vast numbers of persons, as correct. By these, or by some one of them, the mind may become preoccupied until it rests undoubtingly in them as true renderings of the Apostolic thought.

Aware of the doctrinal importance of this Letter, the masters of controversies, in all ages, have felt that they must have on their side the weight of its authority. But in their efforts that way they have not dealt justly with the object of their common desire: possession, at all hazards, would seem to have been the aim. Biassed, by temperament or by education, towards particular views, or confident in respect to the special dogmas of their schools, their labor has been, not to learn by patience and study what God's word doth really teach, but to assert and defend the tenets of their choice and affection by whatever they could lay hands upon, in that vast armory of weapons. Lutheran and Calvinist—the Solifidian and the Antinomian together, have ransacked this precious treasury in haste and fury, each party with the settled assurance that its own theories must be demonstrable thence, or discoverable therein, because each held its own theories to be certainly true. Thus the Scripture has been wrested in support of views respecting which it does not appear that a thought, even the remotest, had ever crossed the Apostle's mind; side issues have been made in the most startling and unexpected way; conclusions, true perhaps in the way of logical inference, have been sworn to as though stated in terms in the text; and the Apostle has been represented as a party to controversies unheard of in the age in which he lived.

It is thus that the mind becomes so seriously embarrassed with reference to this Epistle. For the great subjective Systems of modern date have exerted on Protestant Christianity an influence so powerful, that the ideas presented by them seem to be woven into the texture of the common thought. Men speak the language of those systems, scarcely observing that such is the case; and inadvertently attach to certain words of Holy Scripture the meanings which, in those systems, the same words hold. The Moral Sense, as we know, may become so corrupted, that a man shall scarcely be able to discern between right and wrong: in like manner the Mental Sense may be perverted by commerce with error until the power of recognizing the Truth is seriously impaired. And hence our chief perplexity with respect to this Epistle. It is not merely that the words of the holy Apostle are dark, and that there be in this, as in all his writings, things hard to understand: but, in addition, prepossessions, prejudices and foregone conclusions, have probably occupied the ground; a wrong chord may have been struck; the form of the truth may have been obscured by the mists of neighboring error. We have to deal with minds ignorant of the extent to which they have been misled; with men who think they are in the green pastures and beside the still waters, when their way is through a speculative labyrinth, built by human hands; with those who fancy that they have grasped the thought of a Paul, when they are but conning the gloss of some founder or champion of a modern sect. He, therefore, who would study this Epistle to advantage, ought (if that be possible) to clear his eyes of the film of these many inventions; to forget (if he can) the popular ideas, and even the language in which they are conveyed; to resolve that he will see in the sacred text no more and no less than what is there; and to strike at once for the centre and heart of the truth.

In proportion to the difficulty of the task is the necessity that some one should undertake it, in behalf of the members of our own branch of the Church. For we have had the misfortune to be overlaid by surrounding denominations, and confounded with them. Their distinctive doctrines have been supposed to be also held by us: and shapes have been imagined as seen in the mirror of our Formularies which they did not really reflect. Thus, *e. g.*, it is thought that in one of our "Articles of Religion" the Calvinistic ideas about Predestination are contained; while another is quoted to show us to be one with Luther in his peculiar views of Justification by Faith. And the fact that we have grown so fast has worked us harm; we have received more than we have assimilated. Numbers of persons have come to us, not under a conviction of duty, nor from a persuasion of the divine claim of the Church on conscience and soul, but merely as they were led by chance or choice: and such converts as these, although adopting our forms, remain in heart and belief that which they were. Theirs they bring with them; ours they receive but in part: and the conglomeration of opinion thus resulting threatens damage to the system. In respect to the Epistle now before us, there has been particularly felt that danger which arises from our proximity to error. We need to remind each other and ourselves that the popular lines of interpretation are not the only ones; that they are inconsistent with the principles and practices contained and enjoined in our Book of Common Prayer; and that if we know no other interpretation than these, we must feel an inconsistency between our Formularies and that supposed sense of the Scripture. The author is sure, from his own experience, that no Commentary on the Epistle to the Romans can meet the wants of the Churchman, unless in every part of it the system in which he has been trained be reverently held in view; unless such Commentary harmonize with all the Articles of the Catholic Faith, as he has been taught them; unless the Creeds and Liturgy, the same in all ages, are one with it in temper, and it with them.

Shall it be said that this is to take the very course of which we have complained, and to do that thing to which we objected when done by others? Surely not. To follow individual opinion as our guide is one thing: to be informed by the consent of the Catholic Church is another. The Reason, unaided, has no promise of success in efforts at coming to the knowledge of the truth: but the Church is the pillar and ground of the truth from generation to generation. For her the Scriptures were written; her system was settled, her sacraments ministered, her doctrines taught, her dogmas known and received to the salvation of the soul, before so much as one of the holy books of the New Testament had been penned. Centuries had elapsed since the Ascension of our Lord,

*a**

before the New Testament, in its present form, was universally received. They to whom these books were addressed, or into whose hands they came, knew already what they must believe: and it is not unreasonable to assume that knowledge of the faith should precede the reading of the Scriptures, if they are expected to bring forth their abundant fruit. The thorough comprehension of the System of the Church must surely be regarded as a condition to the profitable study of a work addressed to the Church. And further, since it was the object of the Apostle, in writing, not to introduce to the Romans a Gospel with which they were up to that time unacquainted, but to establish and confirm them in the one which they had already received, so ought we to try all interpretations of the Scripture by the unchanging Faith of the Church, and to reject at once any scheme which ignores that Faith; which contradicts, in any particular, Catholic dogmas; or which cannot be reconciled with the System of Catholic Christianity.

The writer of this following Exposition has been minded so to study his subject as conjecturing the needs of others from what he knew of his own. Aware that the Church preceded the Bible in the order of time; convinced that her uniform testimony to the sense of Holy Scripture must be correct; reverencing her as the Witness and Keeper of the Truth, and as having authority in controversies concerning the Faith, he has sought to read, and to show others how to read, by the bright beams of light which she affords. Her Creeds, and the language of her Sacramental Life, seem to him to be the key to all which is dark in the Written Word. It is not, then, to variable human opinion that they look for aid who desire to hear the Church, but rather to the radiance of that City set on a hill; and, if we refuse the helps which the Lord has given us, we err, and erring must bear the consequences. He who should study the Word with no better aid to the knowledge thereof than that which his understanding is able to afford, may look to fail in the rash attempt; and, if such a man perish in his presumption, the blame shall lie at no door but his own.

It is hoped that whatsoever has been committed to the following pages may be found to accord with the Analogy of the Faith. The writer is little concerned as to agreement with individual teachers; and whether he may or may not be supported by this name or that, is to him a matter of the least consequence. But it were a heavy charge that aught herein contained was out of harmony with the Everlasting Thought of the Catholic Church, or not in full accordance with the tradition of those things which from the beginning have been most surely believed among us; and if such disagreement can be pointed out, none will be readier to admit and deplore it than the writer.

This work is now humbly offered to the faithful of that communion in which it is his privilege to serve as a priest. It has been prepared almost under a sense of duty; but at least with the hope of accomplishing one of the Spiritual Works of Mercy, in guiding the doubtful. It cannot but be most imperfect and incomplete: but if, in the household of faith, it may prove of service to some devout lovers of the Word of Life and of the old things of the Church; if it should avail to help any one to see more clearly that the ways of the Church, as we know them, reflect the Mind of the Spirit; if it should suggest the preparation of some fuller and more worthy work of the kind, in quarters where Leisure, Love, and Knowledge may be found together, the labor expended now will not be counted as lost. And so the writer would commend this, and all undertakings, to the merciful indulgence of the Almighty, that He, the Father of Lights, would grant to His people more and more of that wisdom which cometh from above: unto Whom, with the Son and the Holy Ghost, be praise and glory, world without end. Amen.

NEW YORK: EASTER-TIDE, 1862.

EXPOSITION

OF THE

EPISTLE TO THE ROMANS.

INTRODUCTORY REMARKS.

Of the authenticity and genuineness of this Epistle there can be no doubt. It was written by S. Paul to the Roman Church; and the statements at the end, as to the time of transmission, and the messenger, are correct.

It cannot now be determined by whom the Church at Rome was founded. It must have been of very early origin. A probable theory is, that the Gospel was first introduced in the Imperial City by some of the "strangers of Rome," who were at Jerusalem on the Day of Pentecost.

S. Paul had not yet visited Rome. This letter to the Church in that place was probably composed some time during the three months spent by him in Greece, and mentioned in Acts xx. 2, 3.

Of the general character of this Epistle it may be observed, that there is a difference between the letters addressed by him to Churches where he was personally known, and to those which he had not yet visited. The former have a more familiar and paternal character, abounding in personalities, commendations, censures, or the like. The latter more nearly resemble theological tractates. Such a one is this letter to the Romans: a grand composition, carefully studied, and apt to instruct in the deepest mysteries of the Faith.

S. Peter has remarked, that in his brother Paul's epistles were many things hard to be understood, which they that were unlearned and unstable wrested to their own destruction. Of none could this be more properly observed than of the Epistle to the Church at Rome. It has been perverted, more than any other, from its original meaning. The Lutheran scheme of Justification has been built up of materials quarried out of its heart; the Calvinistic theory of decrees has been forced on the unwilling mind by citations from its mysterious pages; it has been dragged into the midst of the dustiest and angriest arenas of theological strife, and there rent in pieces. The main difficulty in the way of a satisfactory interpretation lies in the prevalence of traditional error concerning it, and in the thickness of the *débris* from earlier and later contentions. The attempt, therefore, to interpret this Letter must be commenced in doubtfulness, and conducted with much diffidence.

Two facts seem to have been forgotten, unnoticed, or unknown by many of the commentators: 1st, that this Epistle was addressed to Human Beings; and 2dly, that the persons to whom it was sent were members of an organized and flourishing Church. It would be impossible for us to accept some of the popular expositions as correct, unless we had, first, disavowed the common convictions of mankind, and, secondly, renounced all that is distinctive in the position of a Churchman. Almighty God has implanted within us certain ideas, which all the race hold in common, and about which there can be as little ground of doubt as about any matters of practical experience. And, secondly, a church—*i. e.*, a branch of the Holy Catholic Church—must, of course, have a faith, a creed, ordinances, and a ministry. It should not, therefore, be forgotten that this Epistle, in coming to the hands of the Romans, would come to men neither destitute of moral ideas, nor yet without a settled belief, but already in possession of that knowledge of God and of themselves, which may be had through the Natural Reason and the Conscience; to men already baptized into the Church of Christ, familiar with the main points of the Gospel, and living in the midst of the ordinary means of light and grace. Therefore, in interpreting this Epistle, we must hearken, first, to the Voice of God, as it speaks to men through the whole frame of Nature; and, secondly, to that same Voice as it is heard in the rites and order of the Church; and any views or expositions inconsistent with either of these voices, we may, and ought to, reject. S. Paul, in addressing these persons, appealed to that knowledge of God which may be had from the things that are made: he also styled them "faithful in Christ." This should intimate our true course and duty in interpreting his words. He teaches no new religion; his treatise confirms and reasserts the Religion of Nature, and adds thereto the power and glory of Divine Grace. He cannot have intended to contradict the convictions of Humanity, nor yet to impugn the System of the Church of Christ.

What, then, is the subject treated of? It is commonly remarked that the holy Apostle discusses two topics: Justification by Faith, and the Catholicity of Redemption. But how does he come to be speaking of those questions? Is there no unity in this composition? Has it no central idea? We suppose that these inquiries may be answered in the affirmative, and that the whole Epistle is a development of one thought.

The Letter is manifestly divisible into two Parts. The first eleven chapters form its doctrinal portion, and the remaining five its practical part.

The key to the Doctrinal Part is in the eighth chapter. In that chapter the Apostle speaks of a certain Purpose and Plan of the Almighty. It is the Plan which is elsewhere mentioned (Col. i. 26; Ephes. i. 9–11) under the title of a "Glorious Mystery." It was conceived from eternal ages; all things temporal have been and are being made to work gradually toward its accomplishment; and it has for its end not merely the fortunes and everlasting condition of men, but those also of angels; things in heaven and things in earth being alike included therein. The Apostle has in other writings of his, spoken of this Great Mystery as constituting the sum and substance of the Gospel. In the Epistle to the Romans, he treats at length of two points in connection with it: viz., of the fact that no man could merit a share in a blessedness so great, and of the certainty that it is intended to embrace all sorts and conditions of men.

From this point of view, let us take a general survey of the train of thought.

The Apostle, after customary salutations, announces as his subject the Gospel of Christ.

We know, from other sources, that the final object of the Gospel is as follows: "That in the dispensation of the fulness of the times, GOD might gather together in One all things in Christ, both which are in heaven and which are on earth." This is "the hope of His calling," and this "the Riches of the Glory of His inheritance in the Saints;" this is the manner of that Future which He promises to the suffering world.

But men must feel their unworthiness of the promised mercy, in order that they may be prepared rightly to embrace the offer. And therefore the Apostle declares that the Good News is for all mankind, and yet that none are worthy to hear it.

First, he proves the unworthiness of the Gentiles. They were not without knowledge of GOD and of His will, for they had the light of Nature. But yet they did not live according to their light. They lost the idea of GOD; they declined to abominable idolatry; they sank into the deepest mire of sin.

Secondly, he shows that the Jews were equally undeserving of this great blessedness which GOD meditates for men. Their means of knowing the Lord and their duty were greater than those possessed by the Gentiles; for they had a direct revelation, known as "the Law." But their System could not save them; for they did not live up to its terms, nor fulfil its conditions. And they to sinful unworthiness had added arrogance and pride; for they had come to entertain the idea of a debt to them, founded on the fact that the Almighty had entered into covenant with their nation; and thus they had lost the idea of His relationship, as a Father, to all mankind.

Thus, men in general are proved to be sinful before God. And therefore they had no right nor title to the promised blessing. Since, then, they could not claim it as a debt, they must be content to receive it as of grace. This is the principle on which God must ever deal with us His fallen creatures.

The Apostle then proceeds to the cause of this general condition. He ascribes that condition to the presence and motions of Sin; and he traces actual transgression to a radical fault and defect in Human Nature, inherited from Adam by carnal descent.

Sinfulness, while it remains, is the barrier between Man and God. It must be removed before the Great Purpose can be accomplished. Man cannot free himself from the plague. God, therefore, has designed and effected our deliverance, by the Mission of His Son our Lord Jesus Christ.

Christ is become a Sacrifice for the Sins of all the world, and by His Atonement, upon the Cross, the original disease of our race is, as to its guilt, entirely removed: God pardons the same forever.

But the Sin, for which Forgiveness has thus been obtained, must also be exterminated from the system. The same Christ, therefore, having died for our sins, was raised again for our justification; He is become a second Head of the Human Race; and men obtain from Him the principle of a spiritual life, more than sufficient to counteract the principle of death inherited from the First Adam; and thereby are they born again to the hope of that blessed and glorious Future.

As all things have been made to work together towards the accomplishment of God's Eternal Purpose, so the various dispensations under which men have from time to time been placed, were intended to prepare the way for their ready acceptance of the Divine System announced under the Gospel. Thus, for example, the design of the Law of Moses was to expose the sinfulness which it had no power to remove, and so to lead towards a thankful acceptance of the Great Redeemer, when He should appear. All, therefore, who, schooled by the bitterness of their spiritual conflicts, will receive the Gospel, shall find therein relief and safety; they shall be made the children of God, and freed forever from the bondage of Sin and Death.

And thus all events of time move slowly but steadily towards the realization of the Mighty Plan, and towards the ultimate triumph of the Divine Love.

Such is the general scope of the Doctrinal Portion of the Epistle. And having thus rapidly glanced at the line of argument and its results, let us next, by way of completing this introductory sketch, turn our attention to some leading words or phrases respecting which the popular errors occur.

Three words, especially, need to be understood, before we can proceed with safety; and those are the three which have been most misinterpreted: they are *Righteousness*, *Faith*, and *Justification.*

It were a task both long and painful, to enumerate the many perversions of these words, each characteristic of some comparatively modern Scheme of theology. The writer prefers, therefore, to state at once the sense of each which he thinks to be true, as tested by Catholic Analogy and Consent; and afterwards to notice some few propositions, which, tested in the same way, are only partially true, or altogether false.

By *Righteousness*, must be understood, first, the Essential Virtue, Holiness, and Excellence of Almighty God. The word is also used to describe that quality in Man which consists in the presence of the Holy Spirit. Righteousness and True Holiness are the same, at last. But in various ways must the term be understood, as applied to God, the Immaculate Son of God, and to Man.

By *Faith*, is meant that act of the human soul, heart and mind, which looks to God alone, and, rejecting self, intends to render full obedience to the Divine Will The term includes whatever Man must do, for his part, toward securing the salvation offered to him by Christ; and the faithful are they who comply with the conditions required of them in the Gospel, whatever those conditions may be.

Justification, in its widest sense, includes the whole benefit conferred upon men in our Lord Jesus Christ. But it is often used for some one part of a complete circle of gifts. For it may signify the first acceptance of the sinner, and therefore, of course, his pardon; since he must be *accounted righteous*, and forgiven, before he can be received into favor. And it includes the idea of a man's *being made* that which he is *accounted to be;* for these two cannot be disjoined but by a technical quibble. So that to be justified sometimes means to be forgiven, and sometimes to be made alive unto God through the Spirit; sometimes to be accounted righteous, and sometimes to be made righteous.

And, in addition, let it be noted that the phrase "*Justification by Faith alone*" does not express or contain a full account of the instrumental or conditional means of Salvation under the Gospel; but that it is a theological definition of the Meritorious Cause of our acceptance. When it is said that a man is justified by faith, it is not meant that his act of belief justifies him or renders him acceptable unto God; nor that his faith is solitary in its office, and has no connection with love, hope, repentance, and obedience; nor that God attaches any higher value to our act of believing, than to any other act or acts which men might perform. But it is meant that a man is accepted of the Almighty, not in respect of any thing that he can do, to purchase salvation thereby, but solely for the sake of our Lord Jesus Christ. The phrase is equivalent to this proposition:—that the Lord Jesus Christ is the only Meritorious Cause of Man's redemption, and that, but for Him and His work, no man could be saved.

Finally, it is necessary to clear the mind of certain errors, ere we proceed; and therefore the following propositions are noted, as being at once, for the most part, popularly accepted, and, at the same time, false. Some of them are false absolutely; the rest are false through defect.

1st. That Justification means only Forgiveness:

2d. That to be justified means to be accounted righteous, but not to be made so:

3d. That Justification and Sanctification are so essentially different as that they ought never to be confounded:

4th. That the only Righteousness which Man needs is the Righteousness of our Lord Jesus Christ, which, by a fiction, is supposed to have been rendered by us; and that we are accepted on the score of that Righteousness so imputed to us:

5th. That Faith is the active instrument towards our acceptance with God, and that it is, in its own sphere, the cause of Man's Justification:

6th. That the Faith required of us unto salvation is, the certainty that we shall be saved:

7th. That whosoever firmly and without doubt believes that he shall be saved, will certainly be saved:

8th. That a man's works contribute nothing toward his justification:

9th. That when it is said that a man is justified by faith only, all other acts, instruments, and means are thereby excluded from the process:

10th. That men could not be saved under the Law, because the Law requires a perfect and absolute obedience:

11th. That the Faith and the Works of the Gospel are essentially distinct; and that Righteousness and Morality are two different things:

12th. That God's Election and Predestination do not contemplate the whole human race, but that they are limited, individual and absolute, instead of being general and conditional.

From these, and all cognate errors, may the Lord, in His Mercy, deliver His Church! And may He bring us back to the ground which we have lost, turning the hearts of the children unto the fathers, and so vindicating Religion from the contempt into which, through the multiplied arts of the Adversary, she has been suffered to fall! And humbly imploring the Divine Blessing, let us proceed to the study of this venerable and satisfying portion of the Word of Truth.

PART FIRST.

THE DOCTRINAL PORTION OF THE EPISTLE.

CHAPTERS I. TO XI. INCLUSIVE.

Section First.

Conviction of Sin.

(Chapter i. verse 18, to Chapter iii. verse 19.)

COMMENTARY.

THE APOSTOLIC SALUTATION,

AND INTRODUCTORY REMARKS.

(CHAPTER I. 1–15.)

1. Paul, a servant of Jesus Christ, called *to be* an apostle, separated unto the gospel of God.

1. Literally, *a called apostle:* and see i. 7, where the Romans are spoken of as "called saints." The Jews were inheritors of God's promises, and had a birthright; but the Gentiles were called to that which they possessed not before: compare Ephesians ii. 11, 12, 13.

"Separated," &c. Set apart for the work of preaching the Gospel.

2. (Which he had promised afore by his prophets in the holy scriptures,)

2. The Apostle would show the Jewish converts at Rome, that he reverences and devoutly receives the Scriptures of the fathers: and also that the Gospel System had been, from the first, intimated in those writings.

3. Concerning his Son Jesus Christ our Lord, which was made of the seed of David according to the flesh;

3. The Jews had a double tradition; that Messiah should be the Son of David, and that he should be the Son of God: yet they knew not how to reconcile the two articles of their belief. (See S. Matt. xxii. 41–46.) But the Apostle shows, that Christ was the Son of God from the first, and that by entering into David's line, He became David's son as to His Human Nature.

4. And declared *to be* the Son of God with power, according to the Spirit of holiness, by the resurrection from the dead:

4. "With power:" an adverbial form, "powerfully," *i. e.*, with manifestations of God's direct agency.

"Spirit of Holiness." 1st. It has been thought to mean the Holy Ghost, and then it must be understood, either "according to the predictions of the Holy Spirit in former times," or else, "according to the miraculous operation of the Holy Ghost after the Lord rose from the dead." But, 2dly, and better, it has been understood to mean, Christ's glorified Humanity; and then there is expressed a contrast between "the Flesh," or that Body of Suffering and Death in which He dwelt among us, in great humility, and "the Spirit of Holiness," or that Body of Immortality and Excellent Glory in which He rose, and ascended, and shall return to judgment.

"By the resurrection." For Christ's Exaltation dates from Easter-Day. And again, the Apostle would remove, by mention of the Resurrection, the offence of the Cross.

5. By whom we have received grace and apostleship, for obedience to the faith among all nations, for his name:

6. Among whom are ye also the called of Jesus Christ:

7. To all that be in Rome, beloved of God, called *to be* saints: Grace to you and peace from God our Father, and the Lord Jesus Christ.

8. First, I thank my God through Jesus Christ for you all, that your faith is spoken of throughout the whole world.

9. For God is my witness, whom I serve with my spirit in the gospel of his Son, that without ceasing I make mention of you always in my prayers;

10. Making request, if by any means now at length I might have a prosperous journey by the will of God to come unto you.

11. For I long to see you, that I may impart

5. "Grace and apostleship:" distinct thoughts; the personal gift, and the official.

"For obedience," &c. To make, in all nations, converts to the faith, who shall, by holy obedience, show its power.

7. "Rome:" the capital of the world and seat of empire. The faithful there, though not much observed by others, were, to Christian eyes everywhere, objects of great attention. The faith of the Church at Rome was celebrated, either from its great vigour and clearness, or from the large numbers who professed it.

"Called to be saints." The term *saints* in the New Testament generally expresses what men are by vocation, rarely what they are in character.

"Grace and Peace." Pass not carelessly by these words: their meaning is deep; the gift of the Holy Spirit, and its result.

10. This Epistle was probably written during the three months mentioned in Acts xx. 3.

11. "Spiritual gift." See 1 Cor. xii., xiii., xiv., on this mysterious sub-

unto you some spiritual gift, to the end ye may be established;
12. That is, that I may be comforted together with you by the mutual faith both of you and me.
13. Now I would not have you ignorant, brethren, that oftentimes I purposed to come unto you, (but was let hitherto,) that I might have some fruit among you also, even as among other Gentiles.
14. I am debtor both to the Greeks, and to the Barbarians; both to the wise, and to the unwise.
15. So, as much as in me is, I am ready to preach the gospel to you that are at Rome also.

ject. The Churches differed greatly in respect to these Charismata; they were most abundantly poured upon Corinth and Galatia. As evidences of the power of the Gospel, the Apostle would have imparted them to the Romans.

12, 13. "Alius longè stilus est apostolicus, atque Curiæ papalis Romanæ." (Bengel.)

14. "Greeks and Barbarians:" a phrase including all the Gentile world. In those days, all were called barbarians who were unacquainted with the language and literature of Greece. (See Acts xxviii. 2, 4.) But nothing contemptuous or offensive was intended in the use of the term: no doubt the Apostle here applies it to the Romans.

The Apostle now proceeds to state the subject of the present Epistle, and to open that subject in order, beginning with the work of convincing all mankind of their state as sinners before God.

SECTION FIRST.

(CHAPTER I. VERSE 16 TO CHAPTER III. VERSE 20.)

CONVICTION OF SIN.

16. For I am not ashamed of the gospel of Christ: for it is the power of God unto salvation to every one that believeth; to the Jew first, and also to the Greek.

16. "Not ashamed." (See Gal. vi. 14.) If the Gospel had been an earthly power, it would have been justly contemptible for its weakness: had it been a human theory, it would have been worthy of rejection for its want of system and philosophic arrangement. But it was neither of these; it was "the power of God."

"The Power of God:" a way in which God acts with power; a powerful instrument in His Hand for saving men from sin, sorrow, and death; and intended, not for a class, but for all the world. "To the Jew first," by inheritance and covenant right, but "also to the Greek."

Observe, that a complete and comprehensive System is spoken of; and every thing which follows in this Epistle, and all that is said elsewhere in the Scriptures, concerning the Gospel, must be understood as of that System, whatever it be.

Remark, also, that in the New Testament there is not to be found, in any one place, a full account of this Divine System of which we speak. Its Nature, its Design, its Organization, its Government, its Laws: we come to know all these by hints, or partial statements, here and there; by inferences from what is written; by traditional information. God's plan of Redemption is worthy of Himself, and it is complete and divine, both in the inner Spirit and in the outward and visible Framework.

17. For therein is
the righteousness of
God revealed from faith
to faith: as it is writ-
ten, The just shall live
by faith.
18. For the wrath
of God is revealed from
heaven against all un-
godliness and unright-
eousness of men, who
hold the truth in un-
righteousness;
19. Because that
which may be known
of God is manifest in
them; for God hath
shewed *it* unto them.

17. "Therein:" *i. e.*, in the great System already mentioned.

The 17th and 18th verses may be taken together; there is a parallelism between them. A twofold revelation comes to us, through the Gospel: 1st, that of God's righteousness; 2d, that of His wrath. Here, also, are contrasted the righteousness of God, and the unrighteousness of men; and this will aid us in determining what is meant by the former term.

The question, then, which first arises is: What is here meant by the Righteousness of God? Some have said that it means "God's method of justifying the sinner." But there is a far more profound and a worthier meaning, in which the narrower one is contained; that it signifies "God's Essential and Eternal Holiness." And why should we stop at lesser senses, when this, the broadest at once and the simplest, presents itself so naturally to the mind and heart? The Apostle's thought seems to be as follows: "That the great and glorious Righteousness of God, with which our unrighteousness lies in such unhappy and hopeless contrast, is brought to light and made more clearly known to the darkened intellect of man, through the Gospel." And why should this be done? Because man, as created in GOD's Image, once partook of that Righteousness; because he lost the gift through the fall; because he cannot be happy until he regain it; because it is the design of the Gospel to make him once more a partaker thereof. It seems as though nothing short of this meaning can suit the grand Exordial Announcement of the Apostle. And the lesser thought is included in the greater. The phrase, "GOD's method of justifying the sinner," if it mean any thing, means naught less than "GOD's method of restoring man to his lost estate, through forgiveness of all his sins, and spiritual sanctification, and bodily redemption in the resurrection at the last day." But these are the ends for which GOD's Nature and Relations to us are revealed.

Let us, therefore, take the word "Righteousness" to mean what it means in Phil. iii. 9, and in this Epistle, iv. 3, 5, 6. And, generally, whenever we are in the face of a great thought, let us rise at once to the highest conception of it which we can find in our minds.

17. "From faith to faith." In the Gospel it is revealed "to faith" (*i. e.*, to be believed by men for their good), that the Almighty will confer the gift of righteousness as "from faith" (*i. e.*, as attainable by men from or through implicit reliance on Him). The Righteousness which GOD gives "from faith" (or, by means of faith), is revealed "to faith" (or, to be believed). So Marriott, on this verse.

"As it is written," &c. By this quotation from Habakkuk ii. 4, the Apostle anticipates a thought, afterward developed at length, that GOD has had but one way of saving men from the very first, *i. e.*, for the merit of CHRIST, and by the road of faith and trust.

18. "From Heaven." A phrase used to enhance the awfulness of the thought. "Hoc majestatem irati Dei significat, oculumque videntem, et iræ latitudinem: quicquid sub cœlo est, et tamen non sub evangelio, sub ira est."

"Who hold the truth in unrighteousness:" who, having means of knowing what the truth is, do not live according to their light, but continue in sin.

Here is a transition: the holy Apostle goes on to show, 1st, that the Gentiles were justly obnoxious to this wrath of God, and this continues to be his subject throughout the first chapter. We need not dwell long on these verses. The picture is horrible, but easily understood.

20. For the invisible things of him from the creation of the world are clearly seen, being understood by the things that are made, *even* his eternal power and Godhead; so that they are without excuse:

21. Because that, when they knew God, they glorified *him* not as God, neither were thankful; but became vain in their imaginations, and their foolish heart was darkened.

22. Professing themselves to be wise, they became fools,

23. And changed the glory of the uncorruptible God into an image made like to corruptible man, and to birds, and four-footed beasts, and creeping things.

24. Wherefore God also gave them up to uncleanness through the lusts of their own hearts, to dishonour their own bodies between themselves:

25. Who changed the truth of God into a lie, and worshipped and served the creature more than the Creator, who is blessed for ever. Amen.

26. For this cause God gave them up unto vile affections: for even their women did

20. "The invisible things of Him," are explained to be "His eternal Power and Godhead."

"From the creation of the world," *i. e.*, from the very beginning; from the very first.

"Are clearly seen." Men may learn of God by study of His works. In fact, there are three ways in which God makes Himself known to us: 1st, through the Consciousness; 2dly, through the Natural World; and 3dly, through His Son. It is one and the same God who showeth Himself in all these ways; but there is no completeness in the former two, and they are meant to lead unto the third and final one. Yet, for all that we have known through them, we are accountable; we shall be judged according to our light.

21. "When they knew God," when they had opportunity and means of knowing Him.

22. "Professing themselves," &c. Either, considering themselves to be really wise; or else, feigning wisdom with a sordid view to gain.

The Apostle now traces the progress of Idolatry in the ancient world; its root is defective knowledge of God, and therefore, until Christ was revealed, and God in Christ, the world was especially prone to that downfall. If man does not worship God as God, he is left to himself, and departs by degrees from that God in whose Image he was made. And then follow, by necessary consequence, the evils here described. For man is "the image and glory of God,"

change the natural use into that which is against nature:

27. And likewise also the men, leaving the natural use of the woman, burned in their lust one toward another; men with men working that which is unseemly, and receiving in themselves that recompence of their error which was meet.

28. And even as they did not like to retain God in *their* knowledge, God gave them over to a reprobate mind, to do those things which are not convenient;

29. Being filled with all unrighteousness, fornication, wickedness, covetousness, maliciousness; full of envy, murder, debate, deceit, malignity; whisperers,

30. Backbiters, haters of God, despiteful, proud, boasters, inventors of evil things, disobedient to parents,

31. Without understanding, covenant-breakers, without natural affection, implacable, unmerciful:

32. Who knowing the judgment of God, that they which commit such things are worthy of death, not only do the same, but have pleasure in them that do them.

(1 Cor. xi. 7.); but God's Image cannot be duly honored where God is not honored. Self-respect and duty to others, grow from the knowledge and love of God.

23. There is a descending climax here. In addition to the kinds of idolatry here mentioned, they went on to worship imaginary monsters, formed of divers incongruous parts: remark the bird-headed deities of Egypt, and consider those fruits of a loathsome syncretism, the centaur, the mermaid, &c.

24. Sin has, as its punishment, 1st, physical miseries, and 2dly, vindictive justice.

28. "Reprobate:" a mind which is thoroughly perverted, which approves the things which it ought to disapprove, and abhors those things in which it should delight.

We will not enter more particularly on the examination of these miserable details: but this is a true picture of Man when he casts off from God.

(CHAPTER II.)

The Apostle has now laid down these propositions:

(*a.*) That the subject of his letter is the Gospel of Jesus Christ;

(*b.*) That it is a System in which God acts with power unto the salvation of men;

(*c.*) That it is effectual to those who believe in it, and accept its terms;

(*d.*) And that the mercies which it bestows are unmerited by mankind.

He has then proceeded to his proof of the last proposition, and, beginning with the Gentiles, he has shown that they deserved punishment, because, although they knew God and His will, they did not live according to their light, but, lapsing into wilful ignorance, declined into all abomination of life and ways.

The Apostle presents the case of the Gentiles first, as being the simpler; and because he would not too early arouse the suspicions or incur the cavils of the Jews; and also because the Gentiles had less light than the Jews, and he would open the subject, logically, from the beginning. But he has said that the Gospel is necessary for all, he must therefore convict the Jews, and this he does in chapters ii. and iii.

He charges the Jews with being also under sin, and guilty before God. But they, for their part, are supposed to urge or offer two excuses or apologies, whereby they fain would shield themselves: the 1st of these he answers in chap. ii, and the 2d in chap. iii.

Let us consider these arguments in order, before we proceed to a literal comment on the text.

The Jew, representative of his race, would speak to the Apostle on this wise:

"What you have said of the condition of the Gentiles is true; they are undoubtedly exposed to the fulness of the Divine wrath. But we, the Israel of the Lord, are safe. The System under which we live is one of covenant with God; there is attached to it a debt. He has entered into agreements with us, and those agreements are perpetual; they are sealed to us and they shall not pass away. In our Law, in our Covenant Privileges, in our Ritual acts and obligations, all of which we punctually fulfil, we remain secure. And so, we need not this Gospel of which you speak."

That this was, in substance, the popular and prevailing idea among the Jews, we know from all that has come down to us, respecting their acts and their history. But the Apostle replies in a simple line of argument, which at once commends itself as conclusive to the mind and the common sense of men. His thought seems to run on this wise:

"God is just. As a Judge, He must be one of perfect equity: He must reward the good and punish the bad. He must judge men, not according to arbitrary distinctions or capricious favouritism, but on principles eternally the same; not according to formal outward conditions, but according to their works and their character. And He must also take into account the extent of each one's knowledge and the advantages which each has enjoyed. These are universal convictions of the human heart.

"Now you Jews have had, what the Gentiles had not, a direct revelation. You have had more light and higher privileges. They had the teachings of Nature, but you have the Written Law. And yet you have done no better, with all your advantages, than they: for you, who judge them, have done the same things which they did. Therefore, are ye also guilty."

This is the line of the argument.

The Gentiles are judged and condemned, because they did not live up to what they knew. They could not plead ignorance, in extenuation of their faults; for they were not left in total darkness, and they ought to have obeyed as far as they could see.

The Jews are judged and condemned, because, having more light and knowledge than the Gentiles, they remained, morally, on a par with them. They could not recur to the privileges of the System under which they lived; because God is righteous, and will judge all men according to their works.

Hence, the need of the Gospel as a means of saving both.

Thus baffled, the Jewish interlocutor or apologist proceeds, in a querulous strain (iii. 1), to demand wherein consists the advantage of being a Jew, &c.

To which the Apostle replies, that the advantage was

great, because the Jews were intrusted with the oracles of God and the fuller knowledge of His Nature and His Will.

Whereupon, the Jew, after some more captious speech, takes this position; that since the oracles had been taken from his people, and given (according to the opponent's theory), to all the world, their unfaithfulness had proved an essential service to mankind, and their errors and faults had become the cause of introducing the nations to all the privileges which were once exclusively their own. Nay, more, God manifests His Righteousness to men, on occasion of their unrighteousness, and the latter becomes a kind of occasional cause of the former. Why then this stern denunciation, either of Gentile or of Jew? and why this Divine indignation against a course which seems to have resulted in good?

To which the Apostle at once replies: That would be to sanction, by implication, the damnable tenet that it is right to do evil that good may come. And since the Jew is reduced to cavils, and to principles abhorrent to the Moral Sense, the argument may be regarded as complete, and the charge is re-asserted:

"All the world is become guilty before God (iii. 19).

To proceed to the examination of the text.

1. Therefore thou art inexcusable, O man, whosoever thou art that judgest: for wherein thou judgest another, thou condemnest thyself; for thou that judgest doest the same things.

The Jews are addressed, through a supposed individual of their number. But yet, what is said is universally true: "They that sin, though they condemn it in others, cannot excuse themselves, and much less escape the judgment of God, whether they be Jews or Gentiles."

"Judge": *i. e.*, censoriously condemn.

"Wherein," &c. He who presumes to find fault with the acts of his neighbour, admits on his own part a knowledge of the Moral Law concerning Right and Wrong; if then he err, he is self-condemned.

2. But we are sure that the judgment of God is according to truth against them which commit such things.

3. And thinkest thou

2. "We are sure:" we know; none can doubt; all must admit, that God is a Judge of perfect equity and truthfulness. Remark how the Apostle appeals to the common sense of mankind · and shall we admit inter-

this, O man, that judgest them which do such things, and doest the same, that thou shalt escape the judgment of God?

4. Or despisest thou the riches of his goodness and forbearance and long-suffering; not knowing that the goodness of God leadeth thee to repentance?

5. But after thy hardness and impenitent heart treasurest up unto thyself wrath against the day of wrath and revelation of the righteous judgment of God;

6. Who will render to every man according to his deeds:

7. To them who by patient continuance in well doing seek for glory and honour and immortality, eternal life:

8. But unto them that are contentious, and do not obey the truth, but obey unrighteousness, indignation and wrath,

9. Tribulation and anguish, upon every soul of man that doeth evil, of the Jew first, and also of the Gentile;

10. But glory, honour and peace, to every man that worketh good, to the Jew first, and also to the Gentile:

11. For there is no respect of persons with God.

pretations elsewhere which contradict, if they do not outrage, that universal conviction?

4. "The riches of His goodness:" *i. e.*, His richly abounding goodness; an amplification very common in Holy Scripture, and especially in S. Paul's Epistles.

5. "Day of wrath." Observe how frequently the Apostle speaks of the last Judgment (for instance, Acts xxiv. 25, and xvii. 31), and how practical a character this gives to his writings. The "Dies Iræ," the great test and proof of each man's work!

6–11. Verses of great importance. They are sufficient, alone, to destroy the Solifidian and Antinomian schemes in all their parts. The last Judgment is spoken of, and the works of men are declared to be the ground of God's acceptance or rejection of them. No one can mistake the Apostle's meaning, nor will subterfuges avail: he speaks strong common sense, and addresses the convictions of all men; but the whole scheme of Imputed Righteousness, and of a mental sentiment or conviction to be accepted in lieu of active obedience, must be felt as utterly inconsistent with these verses. Let us find in them a clue to what comes after; let no interpretation of any other part of the Epistle be tolerated, which does not easily and naturally harmonize with these expressions.

Bengel beautifully remarks, that "eternal life" (verse 7) is an accusative, governed by "will render" (verse 6); but "Indignation and wrath," &c., &c. (verses 8, 9), are not accusatives but nominatives; as if the Apostle refrained from speaking of God as the inflicter thereof: "Horruit Paulus expresse dicere, Deus reddet iis, qui sunt ex contentione, mortem sive æternam perniciem: quare eam rem conscientiæ peccatoris ex antitheto præcedente subaudiendam relinquit: 'Reddet'—non sane vitam æternam! sermonemque flectit adea quæ sequuntur."

12. For as many as
have sinned without
law shall also perish
without law: and as
many as have sinned in
the law shall be judged
by the law;

12. The Apostle having remarked that God Almighty is no respecter of persons, goes on to show in this and the following verses, that He judges and punishes or rewards men according to the privileges they have enjoyed and their means of religious improvement. See 1st Corinthians, ix. 20, 21, for the meaning of "in the law," and "without law:" it means, to express the state and condition of Gentileism and Judaism respectively. "In the final decision, the obligation of the Israelites to obey the law under which they lived shall have its due influence, as shall also that of the Heathen to obey the law of nature, suggested by conscience and reason or traditionary revelation. In a word, the state of each man shall be determined with reference to his situation and advantages." (Turner.)

(13. For not the
hearers of the law *are*
just before God, but the
doers of the law shall
be justified.
14. For when the
Gentiles, which have
not the law, do by nature
the things contained
in the law, these,
having not the law, are
a law unto themselves:
15. Which shew the
work of the law written
in their hearts, their
conscience also bearing
witness, and *their*
thoughts the meanwhile
accusing or else
excusing one another;)

13–15. In these verses the Apostle follows out the thought just expressed. Those shall be accepted with God (justified) who are sincere, and do their best to serve Him.

14. "The Gentiles:" leave out the article; when any Gentile, or Gentiles, &c.

"The Law:" *i. e.*, the written Law which the Jews had.

"By nature:" *i. e.*, in their Gentile condition, without any more direct revelation than that which may be had from the Consciousness and the natural world.

"Do the things:" *i. e.*, do really fulfil the same duties toward God and their neighbour which are contained in the revealed law as precepts of religion.

"Having not the law:" although they have no direct revelation.

"Are a law," &c.: *i. e.*, these convictions take in them the place of a direct revelation, and they are approved of God accordingly if they follow them.

15. "Which shew:" to themselves, to others, and to God.

"The work of the Law:" the efficiency and reality of that Rule of Morality which is eternal in itself, and which God made more clearly known through the Mosaic dispensation; the Gentile who really tries to do right shows that a Moral Law is deeply stamped on his nature, whether he knows aught of it directly or not.

The whole idea is, that "if individuals among the Heathen, living without the advantages of a direct revelation, do in this their natural condition endeavour to live agreeably to the divine law, their own reason and conscience being their governing principle, they show that this law is really their inward guide, though imperfect, and consequently leaving them in a state of indecision, their reflections alternately accusing or apologizing." (Turner.)

16. In the day when God shall judge the secrets of men by Jesus Christ according to my gospel.

17. Behold, thou art called a Jew, and restest in the law, and makest thy boast of God,

18. And knowest *his* will, and approvest the things that are more excellent, being instructed out of the law;

19. And art confident that thou thyself art a guide of the blind, a light of them which are in darkness,

20. An instructor of the foolish, a teacher of babes, which hast the form of knowledge and of the truth in the law.

21. Thou therefore which teachest anoth-

One remark more on these verses. The advocates of the theory of Imputed Righteousness can only avoid the difficulty of the passage by supposing that it is all hypothetical language. But this is a weak and foolish gloss. The Apostle's language is not hypothetical: there were Gentiles, and there always have been, in all systems, men, who, living up to what they knew, pleased God, and were accepted with Him. This passage does not enter into any theological inquiry into the status, or the cause: it is simple speech to ordinary minds. It means, in short, that a sincere Gentile is better than a hypocritical Jew.

16. This must be connected with verse 12, the intervening verses being parenthetical. "Gospel:" The announcement of a Judgment to come,

or, teachest thou not thyself? thou that preachest a man should not steal, dost thou steal?

22. Thou that sayest a man should not commit adultery, dost thou commit adultery? thou that abhorrest idols, dost thou commit sacrilege?

23. Thou that makest thy boast of the law, through breaking the law dishonourest thou God?

24. For the name of God is blasphemed among the Gentiles through you, as it is written.

25. For circumcision verily profiteth, if thou keep the law: but if thou be a breaker of the law, thy circumcision is made uncircumcision.

26. Therefore if the uncircumcision keep the righteousness of the law, shall not his uncircumcision be counted for circumcision?

27. And shall not uncircumcision which is by nature, if it fulfil the law, judge thee, who by the letter and circumcision dost transgress the law?

28. For he is not a Jew, which is one outwardly; neither *is that* circumcision, which is outward in the flesh:

29. But he *is* a Jew, which is one inwardly; and circumcision *is that* of the heart, in the spirit, *and* not in the

is a leading part of the Gospel; therefore, it does not change any of the previous conclusions of men on that subject.

17. "Art called." It was counted a very honourable title.

"Boast:" as though God were thine, and thou God's own.

21–23. Evidently this is a charge which they dared not deny.

24. See Isaiah lii. 5. Ezek. xxxvi. 20. This expression reveals a state of morals little, if at all, better than that of the heathen: even they observed and remarked on the inconsistencies and irregularities of the so-called People of God.

25–29. "Circumcision," in verse 25, means, a Jewish state or condition; "uncircumcision," a Gentile state. In verse 26, "the uncircumcision," means the uncircumcised man.

27. "By nature:" in his natural condition. "By the letter and circumcision:" an idiom of the Greek language; compare 2 Cor. ii. 4, v. 10; and Hebrews ix. 12. It means, in these cases, "in," or "with," expressing condition: and here it signifies, "although enjoying the advantages of the letter," &c.

The Apostle, in these verses, means to say, that the Gentile, who, although he have no direct revelation to guide him, nevertheless fulfils the will of God, so far as he knows it, is in a better and more hopeful state than the Jew, who, in spite of his advantages, continues in wilful transgression. The Apostle is not using hypothetical language, nor supposing a case for the sake of argument. In this

letter; whose praise *is* not of men, but of God.

passage, and generally throughout the Epistle, we should take what he says in its natural sense. Thus, when he speaks of fulfilling the law, he cannot intend a perfect and absolutely faultless obedience; for no one ever rendered such. God requires such an obedience of none of us; He does not command impossibilities. He never, at any time, made perfect obedience the condition of the sinner's salvation. He requires of us a sincere service according to our abilities: and they who render it will be accepted.

1. What advantage then hath the Jew? or what profit *is there* of circumcision?
2. Much every way: chiefly, because that unto them were committed the oracles of God.

It were better that no break were made here, and that the commencement of another chapter were overlooked. For this is the remark of the Jewish objector; a kind of petulant conclusion from what has been said. Convicted by the conscience, the other party loses his temper, and impatiently asks, What then is the good of being a Jew? To which the Apostle replies, that the advantage was great in the mere possession of their privileges: for apart from the use which we make of God's gifts, we ought to be thankful for their possession. The Knowledge of God is the Light of the World, and the hope thereof; and all God's plans are working toward the restoration and recovery of mankind: in their accomplishment He unveils His face by degrees, and, as ages move on, reveals Himself more and more clearly. It is, then, a high and glorious privilege to hold an advanced place in the line of this development, and to be intrusted, as were the Jews, with the charge of the preservation and transmission of any part of the sacred trust of Divine Knowledge. The same objection urged by the Jew, might be urged to-day, as against the value of Christianity: if the heathen, by living according to their light, may be acceptable to God, where is the use of converting them to Christianity? If they can be saved without hearing of Christ, why preach Him to them at all? But how futile and absurd such a thought! Spite of all the danger accruing from increased responsibility, who would not rather be a Christian than a heathen? Besides, among the Jews many may have been led to God by the greater power of the light in them: and life in the world to come may be more excellent by how much better foundation there was laid in this world.

3. For what if some did not believe? shall their unbelief make the faith of God without effect?
4. God forbid: yea, let God be true, but every man a liar; as it is written, That thou mightest be justified in thy sayings, and mightest overcome when thou art judged.

The train of the Apostolic thought continues thus: the infidelity of great numbers can in no way affect the general order and progress of God's designs. His faith, pledged to mankind, shall stand the same, whatever man may do: His promises and calling are facts about which there is and shall be no change; therefore the carelessness, the sin, the unworthiness, of His people the Jews, can never change the state of the case, nor lead us to distrust His perfect fidelity and truthfulness, nor weaken His hold on our submission and His claim to our affectionate service. Be the consequences what they may to men, God's word shall never be distrusted nor disregarded: He is ever one and the same: and if judged, He will always have the advantage. To the Jews were confided the Divine oracles: it was a great and glorious privilege. They proved themselves unworthy of their trust: be it so! God's plans are not changed; His designs shall be accomplished; His Truth shall stand, though not only Jews, but all, proved faithless: His faith pledged to the whole race, Gentile and Jew alike, shall be kept. (Cf. Gen. iii. 15, xv. 5, xxvi. 4, &c., &c.)

5. But if our unrighteousness commend the righteousness of God, what shall we say? *Is* God unrighteous who taketh vengeance? (I speak as a man.)
6. God forbid: for then how shall God judge the world?

The next question is evidently propounded from some such conclusion in the mind as this: That in consequence of the faithlessness of a certain part of mankind, God's mercy had become more widely known. Hence it is argued by the supposed objector, thus: If our iniquities have, Providentially, become the means of introducing this wide and comprehensive Gospel System, wherein the Righteousness of God is commended to men, (why should He take vengeance on us? Does there not appear to be a certain unfairness in it?) This would be the thought, were it carried out: but the Apostle anticipates the objection, and says that to charge God with injustice for taking vengeance on unrighteousness, is to destroy all hope of a Judgment and final vindication of the right. If it were held that sin is not sin, because, in the order of God's moral government, He is able to turn it to good account, all distinction between Right and Wrong, and all judgment between them, would be at an end.

7. For if the truth of God hath more abounded through my lie unto his glory; why yet am I also judged as a sinner?

8. And not *rather*, (as we be slanderously reported, and as some affirm that we say,) Let us do evil, that good may come? whose damnation is just.

The same objection is more formally and nakedly made: "Why should I, the Jew, be condemned and punished, if, through the unfaithfulness which you charge upon me, God's power, truth, and salvation have been so much more abundantly set forth among men? You say, that in consequence of our sin, mercy has been shown to the Gentiles. Well, then, if we had been faithful, the Gentiles would not have been called. Good has come from our disobedience. Why punish us?"

To which the Apostle instantly replies: Such a view, if correct, would exhibit us as holding the principle that the end sanctifies the means, and that men may do evil in order that good may result: which principle is abominable, and the holders thereof are obnoxious to just condemnation.

In order that this passage may be the more clearly understood, from verse 1 to verse 8 inclusive, let it be arranged in the Dialogue form: its parts will then fall into order as follows:

Jewish objector.—What advantage hath the Jew? or what profit is there of circumcision?

Apostle.—Much every way, &c. (through verse 4).

Jewish objector.—But if our unrighteousness commend the righteousness of God?

Apostle.—What shall we say? &c. (through verse 6).

Jewish objector.—If, then, the truth of God, &c. (through verse 7).

Apostle.—Would not this be the same as to say, &c. (through verse 8).

9. What then? are we better *than they?* No, in no wise: for we have before proved both Jews and Gentiles, that they are all under sin;

The objections having been made and answered, the Apostle resumes the general subject. The charge against the Jews, which he had already made, he now establishes and substantiates by the evidence of their

10. As it is written, There is none righteous, no, not one:
11. There is none that understandeth, there is none that seeketh after God.
12. They are all gone out of the way, they are together become unprofitable; there is none that doeth good, no, not one.
13. Their throat *is* an open sepulchre; with their tongues they have used deceit; the poison of asps *is* under their lips:
14. Whose mouth *is* full of cursing and bitterness:
15. Their feet *are* swift to shed blood:
16. Destruction and misery *are* in their ways:
17. And the way of peace have they not known:
18. There is no fear of God before their eyes.
19. Now we know that what things soever the law saith, it saith to them who are under the law: that every mouth may be stopped, and all the world may become guilty before God.

own sacred writings, which set forth the national degeneracy.

9. "Proved:" Better to render it "charged."

"Under sin:" Under the dominion and rule of sin.

11. "Understandeth"—"seeketh."

12–18. These expressions it is best to understand, as having been collected from divers parts of the Holy Scriptures, not as quoted from one place.

S. Paul has adduced these testimonies against the Jews alone: the Law is the accuser of the Jew; Nature condemns the Gentile. Take the first half of verse 19, as a comment on all that he has just said, and the second half as the grand conclusion from all that he has written thus far; it is a summary of the whole section from the 17th verse of chapter 1. This is the proposition which, in that verse, he set himself to prove.

And there and thus the First Section of the Epistle ends.

Section Second.

Salvation by Grace, through Faith.

(Chapter iii. verse 20, to Chapter iv. verse 25.)

SECTION SECOND.

THE Apostle, having completed the work of convicting both Gentiles and Jews of sin, proceeds to speak of its remedy. He has shown, in general, that all are guilty before GOD. He has next to show, in what way men are made acceptable to GOD, through the Gospel of Christ.

In this second Section we recognize one of those places mentioned by S. Peter as "hard to be understood;" it requires very close and conscientious study, lest "they that are unlearned and unstable wrest it to their own destruction." Following the plan proposed, of naming each section, we note as the subject of this,

SALVATION BY GRACE, THROUGH FAITH.

(CHAPTER III. VERSE 20).

20. Therefore by the deeds of the law there shall no flesh be justified in his sight: for by the law *is* the knowledge of sin.

THIS verse contains a general conclusion, from all which has been said.

Now it is of great importance to note, that here and elsewhere, and, in fact, throughout this Epistle, S. Paul refers, not to individuals, but to men in the mass. While condemning Gentile and Jew alike, he is perfectly well aware that in every nation there were some who pleased GOD and wrought righteousness, and that among the Jews there were some of whom it might be said, "Behold an Israelite indeed, in whom is no guile." Therefore, he cannot be understood as referring to particular cases, nor can his words be taken absolutely. He lays down in this verse a proposition, true of men in general, and he is dealing only in wide and comprehensive views of the position, the danger, and the prospects of the race.

The statements in this verse are true of both Jews and Gentiles: but the words will take varied shades of meaning, according as they are applied to each class in turn. Thus, understanding them of the Gentiles, "the Law" means that Moral Law mentioned in ii. 14, 15; and the expression that "by the Law is the knowledge of sin," signifies, in the same connection, that the Gentiles were convinced of their sinfulness by the evident and fatal contrast between their actions and that rule written from the first on their hearts: knowing what was right, yet doing wrong, they stood convicted by their consciences, and aware of impending retribution. Understanding the words, on the other hand, of the Jews, "the Law" must mean that Moral Law, as more clearly revealed in the Mosaic System, together with their entire Religious Code, as well ceremonial as ritual; while it was true of them that "by the Law is the knowledge of sin," because, in addition to the admonitions of conscience, they saw before them, in their services, an ever present picture of the true nature of sin; they were taught that "without shedding of blood is no remission," and they saw the need of a more perfect sacrifice than any which man has to give. (See Heb. x. 1–4.)

Before proceeding with the Commentary, we must pause and reflect; for a difficulty presents itself to the thoughtful believer.

It must be true, that, as was remarked before, the Apostle has been speaking of men in general, and that his words cannot be supposed to extend to every individual case. Among the Gentiles there were righteous men, and this He has admitted (see ii. 14): while, as for the Jews, the same books to which he appeals for proof of their common guiltiness, contain the names and acts of many faithful men and women who were known and declared and accepted as such by the Almighty.

The question might then arise: Could not such as these be saved without the Gospel System? Were not such as these justified through Moral Obedience alone? If so, then must there have been a class of persons saved independently of the Gospel, and there is a possibility of the occurrence of such cases in the future; and thus, the Gospel would appear, however beneficial, to be not altogether essential.

Now, the Apostle does not meet this objection: his language is quite general; and he does not concern himself about conclusions from it. We have, then, nothing in the Epistle wherewith to relieve us of the embarrassment.

In all such cases, the Logical Argument is in order. For although the Mysteries of the Faith are, in every respect, unattainable and undiscoverable by the unaided Reason; yet does not the function of the Reason cease with the reception of Revealed Truth. It is, on the contrary, the proper office of the Reason, to advance from the Axioms of the Creed, toward all such conclusions as may be deduced therefrom. Therefore, although the Apostle does not meet the difficulty before us, yet may it be resolved, by the Reason as illuminated by the Divine Light. When the Intellect applies itself to the study of the Word of God, it perceives continually arising, questions not resolved in the text. On these, the Mind of the Church has ever gladly and actively exercised itself; and, in writings and tractates of inestimable value, we have received from the holy Fathers the results of many efforts on their part to resolve such difficulties, or to investigate the hidden reasons of the mysterious ways of God. The Apostle has stated, of men in general, that by the deeds of the Law no flesh is justified. We may proceed, by a logical argument, to show that proposition to be equally true of every individual. We may appeal to the case of Abraham, as the most illustrious representative of our race in past ages; and, since the Apostle has shown (Chap. iv.) that he was saved by grace through faith, we may argue, *à fortiori*, that no one of us could hope for terms more gratifying to human pride, or else, we may argue, that eternal salvation must either be received as a favour or demanded as a right; that he who would demand it as a right, ought to prove his claim; that such a claim, if set up, ought to be based at the least on the exhibition of a perfect obedience, since it is inconceivable that aught less than this could merit a reward so vast; and that no man has rendered a perfect obedience; so that he who should demand salvation as a right, and who would have the reward reckoned to him as of debt, and not of grace, must fall. But in whatsoever way an argument of this kind might be constructed, it should be advanced as such, retained in its proper place, and not confounded with the direct statements of the context.

It is the more necessary to insist on this, because, either from want of right understanding of the mutual relations of the Reason of Man and the Revelation of God, or from the attaching of undue value to their own ratiocinations, men are perpetually assigning to mere logical arguments the weight and importance which belong alone to the express words of the Holy Spirit. Many of the conclusions which have been drawn from the Holy Scriptures, seem little less binding on the conscience than the Scriptures themselves; and "what can be proved thereby," may be required to be believed. But still, we must discern between the statements of the Scriptures, and our legitimate conclusions from them. This, heretics have not generally done; nor are they prone to do. Rather do they exalt their own arguments or conclusions into the very place of the Written Word, and declare that they are contained therein. Thus, for example, it has been said that no one can be justified by the law, because the law demands an absolutely perfect obedience. This may, or may not, be the reason, but not a word to that effect has been said by S. Paul. Almighty God has never, at any time, required absolutely unsinning obedience of any man as a condition of salvation: nor is the fact that no man has rendered it, assigned in Scripture as the reason why no flesh is justified before Him. The moment we speak of such an obedience, we descend from the infinite position to the finite; we speak as men, and not as of the Lord: our words may be good and useful, but we must take heed lest we say of them, this is the Word of God Himself.

To resume the commentary on the text.

21. But now the righteousness of God without the law is manifested, being witnessed by the law and the prophets:

21. "But now:" A contrast is drawn between past times and the days when all things are become new through the Gospel of Christ.

"Is manifested:" Is clearly set forth as to its origin and nature, its mode of impartation and its results.

"The Righteousness of God without the Law," the Eternal Perfections, Holiness, and Glory, regarded as attainable by man, and as to be enjoyed by him as his highest and perpetual joy; and that "without the law," that is to say, not as having been purchased by him, through any obedience which he has rendered, or has been able to render, commensurate with that inestimable gift, but as once more manifested and revealed, of God's mere and undeserved goodness and mercy, unto all who will renounce, and love, and believe, and obey.

This phrase, "without the law," might be rendered "aside from any claim set up as founded on an assumed obedience." There could not be conceived a more senseless gloss than that which renders it as though there were no connection between Righteousness and Virtue. The Moral Law of God is eternal and unchangeable; and Christ came not to destroy it but to fulfil.

"By the Law and the Prophets" is this Righteousness of God witnessed; an expression which shows that the Righteousness here spoken of is that already described (i. 17), and that our possession of it is in the way of an inner and spiritual gift. (See *e. g.*, Psalm cxix. all through; Ps. iv. 5; v. 13; vii. 8–16; xi. 6–8; xiv. 9; xv. 1, 2; xxvi. 1; cxxv. 4; &c., &c., &c.; Heb. x. 16, 17; Isaiah li. 1, 5, 7; xxxv. 6; xxvi. 2, 3, 7, 9; Hosea x. 12; and the whole drift of Scripture and of the Ancient Fathers.)

22. Even the righteousness of God *which is* by faith of Jesus Christ unto all and upon all them that believe: for there is no difference:
23. For all have sinned, and come short of the glory of God;
24. Being justified freely by his grace through the redemption that is in Christ Jesus:

22. It is here expressly stated, that the gift of the Gospel is a gift of righteousness; that it is the righteousness of God; and that it is "unto" and "upon" men.

"The Righteousness of God:" To render this as if it meant "God's method of saving men," is to give to it one of those tame and weak senses which could never have been assigned to expressions so magnificent, unless men's minds had either been blinded by the dust of controversy, or shaken through fear of error. It signifies no less than the Essential and Spiritual Holiness of Almighty God, so far as man had a share in it by virtue of his creation in the Divine Image, and so far as he is restored to it through the Incarnation and Glorifying of our Lord.

"By faith:" The heavenly gift is granted to all who will believe in God as its bestower, and lovingly desire it.

"Of Jesus Christ:" For He is the Meritorious Cause of our acceptance, and the gift was in Him, and He gives it to us.

23. "For all have sinned:" All are alike undeserving of it.

The Apostle has already proved all men to be under sin, and guilty before God.

If, then, God accepts them, He accepts guilty and disobedient creatures. But how can this consist with His Eternal Justice? And how can men retain due reverence for God, and for His law, while they are thus freely accepted, and while their evil deeds are thus overlooked and forgotten?

And above all, how can the sinful creature be received into communion and fellowship with the Holy Creator?

The knowledge of his sinfulness debars man from claiming salvation as a right; and at the same time, when viewed in connection with what he knows of God, leaves all the relations between the Deity and himself in a state of hopeless embarrassment and confusion.

These difficulties are, however, cleared away by the making known to man his salvation through the Lord Jesus Christ.

For Christ is revealed, 1st, as Crucified; 2dly, as Risen; 3dly, as the Giver of the Holy Ghost.

His Death, is the Price of our forgiveness.

His Resurrection, is the Beginning of our New Life.

His Holy Spirit, is the Agent of a New Righteousness within us.

Through the Gospel, therefore, man knows:

1st. That his sins are all forgiven;

2dly. That the principle of a new life of holiness is already within him;

3dly. That this new life is the work of the Holy Ghost and of Grace.

All that he has to do is, to embrace this Divine System and consent to be saved thereby.

His ground of boasting is entirely removed; for the work and gifts are not of his doing or procuring.

To believe in this Divine Scheme so as to place full reliance therein, and to live thereby, is the faith spoken of by S. Paul.

And "to be justified by faith" means, to be saved for the merits of Christ, in this divinely appointed way.

24. "Justified:" Understand the whole benefit of Redemption through Christ to be meant.

"Freely:" As we cannot claim it, and are, at first, merely and solely, passive recipients.

25. Whom God hath set forth *to be* a propi-

25. The Apostle mentions the first of the gifts of the Gospel, which is of

tiation through faith in his blood, to declare his righteousness for the remission of sins that are past, through the forbearance of God;

26. To declare, *I say*, at this time his righteousness: that he might be just, and the justifier of him which believeth in Jesus.

course forgiveness of sins: first, in the logical order, and first in the order of time. In the process of our Justification, God, if He accept us at all, must accept us as if we were righteous,—must account us to be righteous,—ere He proceeds to make us righteous: therefore the Pardon of Sin (for the past absolutely, and for the future conditionally), is the first gift of Redemption.

25. It was among the results of Christ's Mission into this world, and especially of His Sacrifice on the Cross, that the Essential Righteousness of God was duly vindicated: no remission could be had, save by the shedding of blood: hence the testimony against the unrighteousness of man, which was borne by Christ from and on His Cross, was terribly impressive. This is what the Apostle seems to intend when he speaks of Christ's being set forth as a propitiation to declare thereby the Divine Righteousness, how greatly it had been outraged, how hardly it could be brought back.

26. Thus God remained before the eyes of men the Just and Holy: and thus without compromise of His Eternal Glories and Attributes, He was able to become the Justifier of sinners, *i. e.*, to accept them as if they had been righteous, and to deal with them as such.

27. Where *is* boasting then? It is excluded. By what law? of works? Nay: but by the law of faith.

27. Has any man a right to boast? Certainly, none. We are forever debarred therefrom as much under the Gospel System as ever men were without. Formerly, they were debarred from boasting, by the law of works, none being able to claim salvation on the score of his virtues. Now, boasting is equally excluded; for the Righteousness of man is that which is wrought in him by the Holy Ghost, and he is the mere recipient thereof by faith in Christ.

28. Therefore we conclude that a man is justified by faith without the deeds of the law.

The proposition here laid down by the Apostle as the conclusion from all that he has said so far, has become celebrated in history. Probably no words have ever been more perverted from their original meaning than these. We are concerned, now, solely about their sense as received in the Catholic Church; not with the various sectarian glosses. The Church regards the phrase as a technical one of the highest importance. She denies, however, that it is descriptive of the process of man's salvation. It is intended to state the Meritorious Cause of our redemption. To say that "a man is justified by faith without the deeds of the law," is to say, that he is accepted, not on account of any merit of his own, but solely by grace, and for the Merit of the Lord Jesus Christ. But there is no statement in these words of the Apostle as to the manner of our redemption; the means by which it was obtained; the instruments by which its benefits are conferred and received; or the conditions required of us unto its effectual possession. In fact, the subject of the Justification of the Sinner, fully considered, includes these necessary parts:

1. The Final Cause;
2. The Meritorious Cause;
3. The Formal Cause;
4. The Efficient Agent;
5. The Instrumental Means;
6. The Subjective Conditions.

The proposition of the Apostle defines the Meritorious Cause; it does not include other parts of the subject, much less cover them all.

29. *Is he* the GOD of the Jews only? *is he* not also of the Gentiles? Yes, of the Gentiles also:

30. Seeing *it is* one God, which shall justify the circumcision by faith, and uncircumcision through faith.

29. The Apostle reaffirms former statements as to the universal applicability of the Divine benefit. He has continually in view that grand conclusion so splendidly developed in chapter viii., respecting the Eternal Purpose of GOD togather into one all things in Christ.

"The Circumcision," *i.e.*, the Jews; and the "Uncircumcision," the Gentiles. "By faith.... through faith." Nothing is to be inferred from the change in the preposition; he would say, that GOD will deal with all in the same way, and according to the same principles.

31. Do we then make void the law through faith? GOD forbid: yea, we establish the law.

31. The obligation to Holy Obedience is not lessened, nay it is made stronger. For the sacrifice of Christ displays the sanctity of the Law, which was vindicated by so rare a price, while the gift of that

new Righteousness to man shows that the Law of the Lord is still, as ever, the way of blessedness. "Beati immaculati in via, qui ambulant in lege Domini."

CHAPTER IV.

It would seem to be the Apostle's design in this chapter to meet that error of the Jews before referred to, whereby they held that God, by entering into covenant with them, had both cut off all the rest of the world from hope, and also bound Himself exclusively to them. In chapter viii., the Apostle speaks of the Eternal Purpose of the Almighty, including the Fore-knowledge, the Justifying, and the Glorifying of Mankind (which see in its order fully explained). He would appear desirous to show that man has not bought, and cannot buy, that Glorious Future, but that it is, irrespective of creature-merit, the gift of the Divine Love. It has been from the beginning, held in view by God; and all things have been made to work toward it by a sacred development. In the course of this development occurs the Election of the Children of Israel. But their call to be God's people should never be considered, apart from the place which it holds in the extended plan: it was not for their sakes, but for the general good of mankind; and through it the whole grand result was helped forward, and the way prepared for the coming Christ. But this idea was alien to the Jewish mind: how should the Apostle bring it to their hearts and consciences? He takes occasion of their superstitious trust in Abraham, to explain the circumstances of Abraham's call. He shows of him: 1st, That he was accepted through Grace; and 2dly, That he was made, in God's promise, not the recipient of some limited gifts intended for one small and comparatively insignificant people, but a Head and Representative of many nations. Hence, the Jews might infer: 1st, That the manner of their salvation must be in substance the same as that of the founder of the nation; 2dly, That the dispensation under which they lived was but a transitory one; and, 3dly, That the Gentiles were comprehended in the gracious counsels of God. The Apostle's argument has a two-fold aim: he shows, 1st, That Abraham stood toward the Almighty as a sinner saved by grace; and, 2dly, That the call of Abraham was with a prospective reference to the gathering in of all mankind. That event forms an epoch in history. It is the dividing point between the patriarchal and Jewish dispensations. At that time, and in that act, the purposes of mercy toward our race were proclaimed more widely than ever before since the Fall, or at least more intelligibly. It was an era of expansive good-will toward men. A particular individual was chosen, and to him was repeated the promise of the Redeemer: the abstract began to contract toward the concrete.

Abraham represents the entire family of the saved; the Gentiles, as having been one himself; the Israelites, as having first received the privilege which made his descendants illustrious. From him the moral could be most suitably drawn for the instruction of all. What then was the ground of his acceptance with God? Had he bought the favour which was shown to him? or, was he chosen merely of the grace and mercy of the Lord? The Apostle states, that his acceptance was of Grace; and this he proves by what is stated in the Scriptures concerning him.

But Abraham was a man of such exalted virtue and excellence, as to have been called "the Friend of God." None can pretend to more than Abraham had; therefore none need expect justification on more favourable terms. This seems to be the drift of the Apostle's thought, and Jew and Gentile alike might take it to their hearts. The Gentile could not expect justification through the works of the Moral Law; and the Jew could not forget that Abraham was yet a Gentile when God accepted and called him.

1. What shall we say then that Abraham our father, as pertaining to the flesh, hath found?

1. Both Gentiles and Jews could claim him: for the latter were the "children of Abraham," while the former might regard him as the "Father of the Faithful." Still, the more immediate reference is probably to the Jewish converts, for S. Paul is engaged in endeavouring to remove their prejudices.

"According to the flesh:" In his natural condition. Perhaps there is also a reference to the physical inability of the parents of Isaac.

2. For if Abraham were justified by works,

2. Paraphrase the verse thus: If his justification had been on the score

he hath *whereof* to glory; but not before God.

of works, and not through grace, he ought to have had ground of glorying and boasting: if he could have claimed God's gift, he might have been justly proud of the grounds of that claim. Now, it is true, that as far as other men were concerned, he had ground for glorying, seeing that he was by far the first man of his time, but yet, before God, he had naught to urge, he did not claim the promises on the ground of right and debt, he was but as other men.

Observe, again, that the Apostle is speaking, not of the process, nor of the manner or conditions, but solely of the Meritorious Cause. For S. James tells us that Abraham was justified by works. These two Apostles are speaking of different points in a wide and complex subject: neither of them intended to include it all in a single remark, which, indeed, were impossible. Abraham had the Righteousness of Faith (see commentary on iv. 13); and of this S. James speaks. But that Righteousness, although conditionally necessary and acceptable, is not meritorious; and this is what S. Paul asserts.

3. For what saith the scripture? Abraham believed God, and it was counted unto him for righteousness.

3. In a word, he was saved through Grace, and on the same terms on which any sinner would be saved; and the proof of this lies in the statements of the Old Testament, in which it is said that his faith was what God considered, and that on occasion of that faith He accepted him as if he had been righteous in the perfect sense of the word. His faith was accepted as his righteousness: his faith, with the obedience which it implied, constituted the righteousness which rendered him acceptable before God.

Remark, especially, that "for" does not mean "instead of;" but it signifies "as."

4. Now to him that worketh is the reward not reckoned of grace, but of debt.

5. But to him that worketh not, but believeth on him that justifieth the ungodly, his faith is counted for righteousness.

4, 5. These verses appear to be thrown in, parenthetically, as a kind of comment on the expression last used; they may be thus paraphrased: "Observe what the expression Gen. xv. 6 implies: when it is said of any one that his faith is counted unto him for righteousness, we understand that such a one lays no stress on his works, but simply believes and trusts in the God who justifies the ungodly. The spirit which endeavours to found a claim on its own achievements, must demand salvation as of debt, not of grace. But the spirit of faith in God is the very opposite to this."

4. "Worketh:" *i. e.*, who should work with a view to purchasing Justification thereby.

"Worketh not:" *i. e.*, who (however perfect his obedience, humanly speaking) should have no such idea, nor attach a value to his acts, as meritorious.

These expressions, capable of being grossly perverted, evidently mean precisely this: "the claiming salvation as a due," or "the not claiming it as a due." They are purely technical expressions, and there is much that is elliptical in their cast and turn; but, viewed by the analogy of all this Epistle, they are clear; their meaning, fully stated, is as follows: "If any man should undertake to work up to Justification, in his own strength, and should succeed in doing so, the reward of that labour on his part might be, and would be, claimed by him as a debt; just as a labourer, when his task was finished, would ask for his wages. But these are not they who are saved: the saved are such as believe: and they, although their obedience may have been memorable, and their works many, yet are, in their own eyes, as though they had done nothing, but only seek to be forgiven and accepted, as sinners, by the mercy of God: such are they whose faith is counted unto them for righteousness: and, since that expression is used of Abraham, we know that he was one of these."

6. Even as David also describeth the blessedness of the man, unto whom God imputeth righteousness without works,

7. *Saying*, Blessed *are* they whose iniquities are forgiven, and whose sins are covered.

8. Blessed *is* the man to whom the Lord will not impute sin.

6, 7, 8. A continuation of the quasi-parenthetical observations in the preceding two verses. As much as to say: This same thought is expressed likewise by David in the Psalms, who, in describing those who are blessed and saved, makes mention of them as sinners, and ascribes their acceptance and salvation to the mere and pure mercy of God, representing Him as graciously forgiving them their iniquities, and as no longer regarding them as sinners. The conclusion is, therefore, that Abraham was accepted as a sinner; and that this is implied in the phrase of having faith counted to one for righteousness ; and that this is the blessedness of the state of the Redeemed.

9. *Cometh* this blessedness then upon the circumcision *only*, or upon the uncircumcision also ? for we say that faith was reckoned to Abraham for righteousness.

10. How was it then reckoned ? when he was in circumcision, or in uncircumcision ? Not in circumcision, but in uncircumcision.

The first point may now be regarded as proved : that Abraham was accepted through Grace and Mercy, and that his case indicates the way in which God may be expected to deal with us all. The second point now comes up : whether the Call of Abraham was with a view to the exaltation of one people ? or whether it had a reference to that Divine Purpose which embraces all sorts and conditions of men ?

9. "This blessedness :" The reference is to the Psalm just quoted ; that quotation was made with a reference to the justification of Abraham ; that act, in its turn, had reference to the way and means of life for all.

"The circumcision only :" *i. e.*, was it only intended for Israel ?

"Also :" Understand after this word, an answer, affirming the latter alternative. "For" resumes the subject, and commences the proof that the Gentiles also were held in view.

11. And he received the sign of circumcision, a seal of the righteousness of the faith which *he had yet* being uncircumcised : that he might be the father of all them that believe, though they be not circumcised ; that righteousness might be imputed unto them also :

10. The blessing was granted to him when he was a Gentile, and in a Gentile condition ; and it was not until afterward that the Covenant, whereof circumcision was the sign and seal, was made with him. Therefore, the ground of his acceptance lay not either in that covenant, nor in the sign and seal thereof : they came afterward, but he was accepted, irrespectively of them, and before they existed.

11. Circumcision was the sign and seal of "the Righteousness of Faith," which righteousness he previously had. (See iv. 13.)

"That he might be . . . . :" God sanctioned thus formally His acceptance of that man's faith, and gave to him so solemnly a seal and sign of that acceptance, for the instruction of all succeeding generations, and in order that Abraham might be the model, example, and ancestor, 1st, of all Gentiles who believe, and whose faith is capable of acceptance as his was, and who, like him, may have it so counted unto them; and 2dly, of all Israelites who are sincere, and who not merely have the outward sign, but are, inwardly, the sanctified men which, according to their vocation, they ought to be; who are faithful, *after* being received into the covenant, as Abraham was *before;* and thus He constituted him the spiritual progenitor of all the saved by grace.

12. And the father of circumcision to them who are not of the circumcision only, but who also walk in the steps of that faith of our father Abraham, which *he had* being *yet* uncircumcised.

13. For the promise, that he should be the heir of the world, *was* not to Abraham, or to his seed, through the law, but through the righteousness of faith.

13. "Heir ....:" *i. e.*, possessor. Abraham is here said to be heir of the world; but Christ, in Heb. i. 2, is said to be heir of all things. The phrase is a Hebraism, and expresses pre-eminence, distinction, headship; the reference is still to the Eternal Purpose mentioned in viii. 28, 29.

"The promise ....:" An innumerable progeny was promised him; thus he was to be the Father of vast multitudes. But the promise, as S. Paul explains in Galat. iii. 15, is to be understood of Abraham's spiritual progeny, *i. e.*, of those of whom the Apostle has just spoken, in verses 11 and 12.

"Law .... Faith." The Law should here be understood to mean the Jewish System, as also in verses 15 and 16.

13. "The Righteousness of Faith." This is what Abraham had, and what made him acceptable to God. Throughout this Epistle, three Righteousnesses are spoken of, as follows:

1st. The Righteousness of Works;
2dly. The Righteousness of Faith;
3dly. The Righteousness of God.

Let us consider these somewhat more at length.

1st. The Righteousness of Works, called also the Righteousness of the Law, is that righteousness of a man's own, which ought to be exhibited by him who would claim salvation as a debt. That no one can be accepted with God on the score of such a righteousness, seems evident when we consider the common infirmities of nature, and the entire history of men.

2dly. The Righteousness of Faith, is the Moral obedience of men, rendered of a pure and honest belief in GOD's Word, and in their duty toward Him, but without the thought of claiming any thing of Him as a debt. Abraham, in leading an humble and godly life as far as he knew how to do so, had this Righteousness of Faith. And every Gentile, who, having not the law, does by nature the things contained in the law, has the Righteousness of Faith. It is not meritorious, in any wise: it is merely the result of the attempt to follow the conscience and the teachings of GOD so far as they are manifested to us. This righteousness the Lord accepts, and renders it available for Justification.

3dly. The Righteousness of GOD, as described in iii. 21, 22, is the distinctive Gospel gift and grace. It is given to those who have already the Righteousness of Faith: and it consists in the spiritual union of the believer with Christ, through the power of the Holy Ghost, and his restoration that way to the Image of GOD.

No one but our Lord ever had the Righteousness of the Law: His obedience was perfect.

But every one who wishes to become partaker of the Righteousness of God, must have the Righteousness of Faith as a condition.

14. For if they which are of the law *be* heirs, faith is made void, and the promise made of none effect:

15. Because the law worketh wrath: for where no law is, *there is* no transgression.

14. "They which are of the Law . . . . :" He means the Jews.

"Faith . . . . :" *i. e.*, probably, the plighted faith of God, as in iii. 3; and then the correspondence between "faith" and "the promise" is complete. Or else the sentence may be understood thus: "they which are of the law," may mean, not Jews merely, but Jews who depend on the Law as the means of obtaining the blessings of acceptance and salvation; and then it implies, that if such a course as theirs secures for them acceptance, the principle of acceptance and salvation through grace must necessarily fall to the ground. (But this blessing cannot come in this way), for thus we should be brought under a System of Law the only result from which must be to make us obnoxious to wrath; for where *law is*, there is transgression; and where transgression is, *there* is wrath.

The whole passage is obscure. But yet the 15th verse, however difficult to adjust, does not affect the understanding of the general tenour of the passage.

16. Therefore *it is* of faith, that *it might be* by grace; to the end the promise might be sure to all the seed; not to that only which is of the law, but to that also which is of the faith of Abraham; who is the father of us all,
17. (As it is written, I have made thee a father of many nations,) before him whom he believed, even God, who quickeneth the dead, and calleth those things which be not as though they were.

16. "Therefore . . . . :" understand thus: "Consistently with what has been said, the benefit is granted to faith, and so is perceived to come by favour, not of debt."

"To all the seed . . . . :" *i. e.*, to Gentiles as well as to Jews.

"That which is of the Law . . . . :" the descendants of Abraham by direct lineal derivation as Israelites.

"That which is of the faith, ... &c. :" the descendants of Abraham in fidelity and spiritual character.

"Who is the Father of us all before God. . . . . " Either who was, in God's right, the Father of the Faithful, when as yet those nations did not exist. Or else, who stood before God, in his times, as the great Representative Father of all believers, whom God then foreknew.

17. "Quickeneth . . . . :" reference to what follows in verse 19. "Mortui non sunt Deo mortui : etiam quæ non sunt, Deo sunt."

18. Who against hope believed in hope, that he might become the father of many nations, according to that which was spoken, So shall thy seed be.
19. And being not weak in faith, he considered not his own body now dead, when he was about an hundred years old, neither yet the deadness of Sarah's womb:

18. Note that the faith to which justification is ascribed is not a small thing but a very great power. Observe also the peculiar moral significance of this case: life shall come out of a dead thing: the human faculty or vessel, which is of itself utterly powerless, shall yet become alive by the aid of God: and it is on the Divine Power, as contradistinguished from the Human, and as needed to supply its deficiencies and give it vitality, that Abraham is required to believe. His dead body may well represent the Nature of our fallen race: the seed or offspring which it bears is like the Righteousness which cannot be attained by any unaided efforts of ours: and God's interposition is that to

which all the work is due. Here, in symbol, is the whole lesson contained.

20. He staggered not at the promise of God through unbelief; but was strong in faith, giving glory to God;

21. And being fully persuaded that, what he had promised, he was able also to perform.

22. And therefore it was imputed to him for righteousness.

23. Now it was not written for his sake alone, that it was imputed to him;

24. But for us also, to whom it shall be imputed, if we believe on him that raised up Jesus our Lord from the dead;

25. Who was delivered for our offences, and was raised again for our justification.

21. "Able;" and of course, willing.
23. The fact of Abraham's possessing
the righteousness of faith, was not
recorded to eulogize him, but for
24 the encouragement and comfort
of all believers to the end of time,
and specially for the carrying out
of the Grand Purpose and Design
borne in mind from the very first.
Belief in the Lord God as the Giver of Life, is implied in the believing on Him that raised up Jesus from the dead.

25. In this verse the Lord is spoken of as having been a sacrifice for sins, on His Cross, and as being the Author of Justification in His Resurrection. Again let it be observed, that Justification signifies the whole benefit of which God makes the Faithful partakers in Christ Jesus; that it is herein especially connected with the Lord's Resurrection; and that the Resurrection was the great and first theme in all the Apostolic preaching. These considerations will save us from the common error, that Justification means Forgiveness alone.

Section Third.

Method and Means of Salvation.

(Chapters v., vi., vii., viii.)

SECTION THIRD.

A THIRD Section of the Epistle now commences. In the 1st, the Apostle convicts the whole world of Sinfulness before GOD. In the 2d, he states that Salvation is offered to all men without distinction, and that it is of Grace, through Faith. He now proceeds to speak particularly of the manner in which that Salvation has been effected for us; and especially of the Work of our Redeemer. The 5th, 6th, 7th, and 8th chapters of the Epistle contain, as their leading topics, the Atonement of our Lord; His Resurrection; the Death and Burial of Believers, into Him, in Holy Baptism; the New Life of Grace; and the Work of the Holy Spirit. We also must observe that, in the 5th chapter, the Death of our Lord is principally spoken of; that the subject of the 6th is His Resurrection, and our Baptism; and that the operations of the Holy Ghost are especially dwelt upon in chapters 7th and 8th. But these three Divine Mysteries, to wit, the Death of the Lord, His Rising again, and the Mission of the Comforter are, as has already been shown, the three truths of the Gospel, whereby all the embarrassments and perplexities of the penitent sinner's mind are relieved and removed. With the utmost propriety does the Apostle proceed to enlarge upon them. Now these three Divine and Blessed Mysteries constitute in themselves the Entire and Complete Remedy for the sinfulness which, in the 1st Section, the Apostle has proved as existing in mankind, as well as the Effectual Means of that salvation, which, in the 2d Section, he has described as imparted to the sinner. The 3d Section, as a complete and homogeneous portion of this work, shall be held to comprise chapters 5, 6, 7, and 8, under the general appellation of the Method and Means of Salvation; and of this Section there shall be made a subdivision into four parts, the 1st being the 5th chapter, and referring to the Atonement; the 2d being the 6th chapter, and referring to the Resurrection; the 3d being the 7th chapter and the 8th to verse 31, and setting forth the powerful and characteristic Work of the Holy Ghost; while the last nine verses of the Section may be taken as a closing Doxology of praise and adoration, piously and naturally winding up and finishing the whole discussion thus far.

The heading of this Section will then be as follows:

METHOD AND MEANS OF SALVATION.

(Chap. v., vi., vii., viii.), including:

Part 1*st* (chap. v.), *Christ's Death the Atonement for the Sin of Mankind.*
Part 2*d* (chap. vi.), *Christ's Resurrection the Source of a New Life for Man.*
Part 3d (chap. vii., viii. 30), *The Work of the Holy Ghost unto Acceptable Righteousness.*
Part 4*th* (chap. viii. 31–39), *Benediction and Praise of God for all His Mercies.*

METHOD AND MEANS OF SALVATION.

Part 1*st. The Atonement of Christ takes away the Sin of the World.*

(CHAPTER V.)

1. Therefore being justified by faith, we have peace with GOD through our Lord Jesus Christ:

"Therefore....:" a word expressive of transition, and suitable to this commencement of another section.

"Being justified by faith ....:" equivalent to being saved by grace, and not as if it were of debt.

"Peace....:" we are no longer enemies (see verse 10), nor do we fear the anger of GOD (see verse 9).

2. By whom also we have access by faith into this grace wherein we stand, and rejoice in hope of the glory of GOD.

"Access....:" a way of approach: the Cross is the way whereby we draw near to the full grace of the Church in her Sacramental System.

"Stand ....:" *i. e.*, stand secure.

"Rejoice ....:" in the orginal the word signifies, "we boast;" the sense is the same in the 3d verse, and also in the 11th, where it is rendered, "we joy in GOD." All these words carry us back at once to verse 27th of the 3d chapter, where "boasting" is excluded: the sense may be taken as continuous. By nature we cannot boast; but under the Gospel we may, as here explained.

3. And not only *so*, but we glory in tribulations also: knowing

"Tribulations ....:" A remark which was, perhaps, made because of the charge against Christianity that it

that tribulation worketh patience;
4. And patience, experience; and experience, hope:
5. And hope maketh not ashamed; because the love of God is shed abroad in our hearts by the Holy Ghost which is given unto us.

had no marks of God's favour in outward prosperity. Their sufferings produced a patient frame of mind: that patient spirit of acquiescence in God's will furnished the proof of His Power to sustain them: that proof of the sufficiency of God's Grace here, led to the hope of a future and complete deliverance from all evil; and that hope was not such as to disappoint those who cherish it, making them to blush for having, as it were, indulged a vain expectation; but it was a firm and certain confidence resulting from the knowledge of God's Love toward man, and from the love of God which the Holy Ghost infuses in the hearts of the faithful.

6. For when we were yet without strength, in due time Christ died for the ungodly.
7. For scarcely for a righteous man will one die: yet peradventure for a good man some would even dare to die.
8. But God commendeth his love toward us, in that, while we were yet sinners, Christ died for us.

The argument for the full assurance of our hope in God is, that He loved us while we were yet sinners, and that He gave us His Son to die for us while we were yet ungodly. The Love of God vastly exceeds the affection of mortals which is called by that same name. For it would be hard to find a man who would die for a righteous person; although for a good man, in the highest and fullest sense of the word, some one might perchance be found who would die. But Christ died, not for the Righteous, still less for the Good (for men are neither the one nor the other), but for a sinful and iniquitous race. How great is Love like this!

7. "Righteous. . . . Good:" there is a difference between these terms. The latter conveys a higher sense than the former. The Righteous man is one who lives according to rule, and, as respects his fulfilment of duty toward God, his fellow-men, the state, &c., is blameless; still such a person, however strictly honest, and however faultless in his integrity, might, either through an unsympathetic disposition, or through reserve, or distance of manner, fail to attract the warm personal attachment of others, who yet conceded to him their respect and confidence. The "Good man," however, is he who makes himself not merely respected, but tenderly and warmly loved; who influences

not only the intellects of men, but also, and perhaps even more strongly, their hearts. See, for meanings of the word "righteous," 2 Samuel iv. 7–11; 1 Kings ii. 32; and for the meaning of the word "good," S. Matthew xix. 16–17; Acts xi. 24.

9. Much more then, being now justified by his blood, we shall be saved from wrath through him.
10. For if, when we were enemies, we were reconciled to GOD by the death of His Son, much more, being reconciled, we shall be saved by His life.
11. And not only *so*, but we also joy in GOD through our Lord Jesus Christ, by whom we have now received the atonement.
12. Wherefore, as by one man sin entered into the world, and death by sin; and so death passed upon all men, for that all have sinned:

If then GOD did all this for men in their sinful and utterly ruined and lost condition, how much more will He do for them now they are accepted and received as His own!

"Reconciled . . . . :" *i. e.*, by the Atonement offered by Christ on His Cross.

"Saved . . . . :" *i. e.*, made partakers of His gifts of grace and the hope of glory, by

"Life:" the Resurrection of our Lord and the consequent glorifying and translation of Humanity in Him.

11. "We joy . . . . " See remark on the word "rejoice," in verse 2d of this chapter.

The Apostle now proceeds to speak of the calamities which came upon mankind through the transgression of Adam, and to contrast them with the blessings received through Christ. Again, as in the first Section he speaks of the Human Race in general; and he distinguishes, in a style which reminds us of 1 Cor. xv., between the First and the Second Heads thereof, the First Adam and the Second; the one, the Author of Death, the other, the Fountain of Life. It is also clear why this subject is here introduced: it is in accordance with the second of the great themes of which he is treating, the Catholicity of Redemption. He has shown that all the world is guilty before GOD, and that Salvation is by grace, unto all who will accept the terms: now it is right that he should trace that guiltiness to one head, while he develops the power of the Death of Christ toward its removal. Observe, also, that whereas in the 1st Section he has spoken of Actual Sin only, he now refers to a darker evil, viz: Original Sin. Before, he spoke of the transgressions of Gentiles and Jews: now, he refers to that common disease, the same in all men, whence transgressions and offences spring. And this adds weight to all that has gone before.

"Wherefore . . . . :" in continuation of this subject of Sinfulness and its Remedy.

"By one man . . . . :" *i. e.*, Adam. Why was not Eve mentioned? Because, 1st, it was to Adam that the command was given. 2dly, Adam was the head, not only of his own race and offspring, but also of Eve. 3dly, if Adam had not regarded her voice, he would have escaped all that followed.

"Sin . . . . :" what is known in theology as Original Sin is here meant: the tendency, the root, whatever it be, from which result inevitably all acts of sin. But there is no reason why we should not here understand the whole great evil, in its progressive grades; Original Sin, Actual Sin, and Habitual Sin: or, in other words, Moral Depravity, with its necessary results in the form of positive sins.

"The world . . . . :" The Apostle is here speaking of the human race, and not of the Creation in general: Death must have existed previously. When sentence was threatened upon Adam, Death is spoken of, as though the term were understood by him, and needed no explanation; various genera and species of animals had felt it; but then it was announced as likely to be inflicted on the Human Race, previously exempt.

"Death . . . . :" This, like "Sin," above, has a general meaning. It includes all the maladies and miseries which precede Death and herald its approach. For these partake of the nature of Death. Sinfulness and Misery are here spoken of as connected. "Through moral depravity, developing itself in actual sins, and entailed on Human Nature by the fall of Adam, came human misery, physical and spiritual."

"Death passed upon all . . . . :" All became subject to Mortality and Decay.

"And so . . . . :" This establishes the agency of the First Adam in all that followed.

"For that all have sinned . . . . :" Inasmuch as all have become sinful.

13. (For until the law
sin was in the world:

These verses present great difficulty: not so much in their contents as in

but sin is not imputed when there is no law.
14. Nevertheless death reigned from Adam to Moses, even over them that had not sinned after the similitude of Adam's transgression, who is the figure of him that was to come.

their connection with the rest of the Section or chapter.

The first remark to be made is this: that verses 13–17, form a parenthesis. The 18th verse is but a repetition of the 12th. If this parenthesis were not here, there would be no difficulty at all in the rest of the context. It would, therefore, seem as though somewhat of special and particular application were intended here; and the main difficulty is to know why the Apostle introduced the parenthesis, and what caused him thus to diverge from the direct prosecution of his subject. However, this parenthetical manner is not the least characteristic of the Apostle's peculiarities of style.

"For, until the Law:" that is to say, during the interval of time between Adam and Moses, between the Fall of Man and the Covenant made with the Israelites at Mount Sinai, Sinfulness existed among men, "Sin was in the world. Sinfulness, with its consequence, "Death, reigned," lorded it over men, "from Adam to Moses." To what shall this deplorable condition be ascribed?

Observe, that the Apostle must be referring to the Gentiles. For the state of the nations of the world before the Giving of the Law on Mount Sinai, and that of the Gentiles at and after the coming of Christ, may be regarded as one and the same. The Israelites form, in history, a kind of Episode; before them are all the Gentile world: after them are the Gentiles of the latter age: and beside and around them, even in their own times, lay, on every side, the Gentiles in mass. Now it is of this great bulk of mankind that the Apostle is speaking. He shows that there was a fault and corruption of nature in the entire race from the time of Adam; that Sorrow and Death among them were due to that condition; that it was derived from the First Man; and that the Gift and Grace of God are equally, and more, abundant for the reparation of that evil.

Let us therefore explain the passage thus:

13. "For until the Law, sin was in the world:"

For, before the giving of the Law to Israel, all through the past ages, Sinfulness existed, and brought forth its baleful fruits. But what Sinfulness do I now refer to?

That common Sinfulness, whereof I have already convicted both Gentiles and Jews as being under its influence; but of which I have not yet shown how deeply seated an evil it is. For this is more than the Guiltiness arising from

"But sin is not imputed when there is no Law."

transgression of the Mosaic Law: until that Law was given, God could not count men as sinners, and deal with them as such, according to its terms. Yet He did so account them, and did so deal with them, from the beginning of the world, before that

14. "Nevertheless, death reigned from Adam to Moses,"

Law on Sinai was given to Israel. Therefore, since Death held all under his dominion, during the whole period from the Fall till the establishing of the Israelitish Covenant, and since effects presuppose adequate causes, the Sinfulness which thus exposed mortals to destruction must have been something different from the transgression of the Law as Jews understand it. They sinned without law, and perished without law, in those days, as has been said (chapter ii. 12): that is, without a direct revelation from God. The cause then was the Original Fault and corruption of our common nature, in which

"After the similitude of Adam's transgression,"

respect there is no distinction whatever among men. Death, in its reign over mortals, was upon them after the similitude of Adam's transgression: for the Disobedience of Adam was the Cause by which all human kind after him became defiled; and

"Even over them that had not sinned."

there was no exception at all, not even in the case of those who died before committing actual sin. Such, then, were the consequences of Adam's Disobedience, and such is the extent of that Original Sinfulness and Depravity which all inherit by generation and descent from him.

In addition to the paraphrase which has now been made, it needs only to be remarked, that the construction by which the words, "after the similitude of Adam's transgression," are connected with the preceding words, "death reigned," and not with the words, "over them that had not sinned," is the construction put on the passage by S. Chrysostom. The sense is made clearer, and a most perplexing question is avoided as to the kind of transgression which is after the similitude of Adam's offence. S. Chrysostom's words are as follows: *ὅτι οὐκ αὐτὴ ἡ ἁμαρτία τῆς τοῦ νόμου παραβάσεως, ἀλλ' ἐκείνη ἡ τῆς τοῦ 'Αδὰμ παρακοῆς, αὐτὴ ἦν ἡ πάντα λυμαινομένη. καὶ τίς, ἡ τούτου ἀπόδειξις; τὸ καὶ πρὸ τοῦ νόμου πάντας ἀποθνήσκειν ... πῶς ἐβασίλευσεν; ἐν τῷ ὁμοιώματι τῆς παραβάσεως 'Αδάμ.* Quomodo regnavit? in similitudine transgressionis Adam. So, the holy Father. See S. James iii. 9, for a use of this word similitude. Death reigned over men, on their coming into the similitude of the sinner and transgressor Adam.

"Who is the Figure of Him that was to come." The First Adam was a figure, type, or symbol of the Second, inasmuch as each was a head of the race: the evil brought in by the first, was equalled, or surpassed, in extent by the good which came through the Second. Adam was a Figure of Christ, in respect of the universality of his relation to the race.

15. But not as the offence, so also *is* the free gift. For if through the offence of one many be dead, much more the grace of God, and the gift by grace, *which is* by one man, Jesus Christ, hath abounded unto many.

In verse 14 he shows the Similarity between the First Adam and the Second: the one is, to all descended from him naturally, the author of death; the other is, to all new born from Him, the Author of Life. Now he proceeds to show the Difference. For, as S. Chrysostom says, Sin and Grace, Death and Life, the Devil and God, are not equal: but the interval between them is very great.

"The offence . . . .:" the lapse, the fall, the transgression of Adam. "The free gift. . . .:" the blessing given through Christ.

"Many. . . .:" literally, "the many," meaning all the race.

"One Man . . . .:" the Incarnation is here referred to: death came through this nature of ours, and so doth life.

"Much more," &c. Great is the difference between the Grace of Christ and the Sin of Adam: for the former confers upon us much greater benefits, and more numerous, than were the evils brought upon us by the latter: for the sin took away life; but the Grace of the Lord gives back that life, and adds thereto many gifts of the Holy Ghost, together with immortality and glorifying in the Kingdom of Heaven. Adam harmed us less, than Christ hath benefited us.

16. And not as *it was* by one that sinned, *so is*

16. The gift of Christ is not like the Sin of Adam, in another respect: for

the gift: for the judgment *was* by one to condemnation, but the free gift *is* of many offences unto justification.

by the Sin of Adam we became obnoxious to original sin alone, whereas by the Grace of Christ we are freed not only from the condemnation due to that, but also from all other sins of actual transgression; and thus the effect is greater. This explanation is offered in the way of suggestion: the verses are hard to comprehend. The Apostle is evidently contrasting and comparing the losses in the First Adam with the gain in the Second; and, however we may decide to interpret particular expressions, the idea is clear, that the benefits received by mankind in Christ must be counted as overbalancing the evils sustained in the first transgressor. Doubtless the mystery will be cleared up, when "we shall see Him as He is," and when the veil between this world and the next shall be drawn aside; but probably not before. Only after the Resurrection can the fulness of Christ's power and glory be known.

17. For if by one man's offence death reigned by one; much more they which receive abundance of grace and of the gift of righteousness shall reign in life by one, Jesus Christ.)

18. Therefore as by the offence of one *judgment came* upon all men to condemnation; even so by the righteousness of one *the free gift came* upon all men unto justification of life.

19. For as by one man's disobedience many were made sinners, so by the obedience of one shall many be made righteous.

Here the paragraph must be resumed. The first half of the verse is but a repetition of what was said in verse 12.

"The Righteousness . . . . :" This must include as well our Lord's holiness of Person and Nature, as His active Obedience.

"Condemnation . . . Justification." The words must be taken, with all which they imply: the condemnation of Adam conveys to us the idea of his sentence, and also of all its consequences, Misery, Sorrow, Depravity, Physical and Spiritual Death. So the word Justification expresses, 1st, the act of Pardon and Forgiveness, and then includes the gift of the new life, the sanctifying and cleansing of the inner man, as well as the sealing the mortal frame for a blessed and happy resurrection. This is more clearly expressed in verse 19. How are we made sinners by the disobedience of Adam? As inheriting by carnal descent, from him, a dying nature. And so we receive the germ, the seed, the principle of the Righteousness of God, by vital and organic union with the Risen and Glorified Christ. To render the terms "made sinners," and "made righteous," in these verses, as though they meant, "dealt with as sinners," and "treated as righteous," is to fall to a low and common meaning, unsuited to the loftiness of the subject, or the importance and grandeur of the language and its applications.

20. Moreover the law entered, that the offence might abound. But where sin abounded, grace did much more abound:
21. That as sin hath reigned unto death, even so might grace reign through righteousness unto eternal life by Jesus Christ our Lord.

20. "The Law . . . . :" There is no article in the Greek: let us then take the word as expressing, simply, *Law;* not the Law of Moses; but the Statute of God, which is forever the same, and of which the language is, "the soul that sinneth, it shall die."

We must also supply an ellipsis to make the sense complete: the thought will run thus: Sin entered into the world: Law, thereupon entered (stealthily and unexpectedly crept in, as the original has it); not that men might be made worse, but in order that, as a consequence, a fuller consciousness and conviction ot the presence of Sin might take effect among men, and that in multitudinous instances it might be exposed. And the same thing was yet more true when the Mosaic covenant was made: for in its rites and offices, a yet fuller representation of the exceeding sinfulness of Sin was made before the eyes of men. Thus the offence abounded: so that all the earth was filled with the knowledge of its nature and its results. But where Sin was thus revealed in all its strength, Grace was even more conspicuously set forth as the remedy.

"That the offence . . . ." &c. This is not to be understood as expressing a reason why, "in order that," but a result, "so that."

METHOD AND MEANS OF SALVATION.

Part 2d. Christ's Resurrection the Source of a New Life for Man.

The whole life of Man is embraced under the heads of a Past, a Present, and a Future.

The first gift of Salvation under the Gospel relates to the

Past. It is that of Forgiveness. And that Gift is more particularly connected with the Cross: for the Death of our blessed Lord was the Atoning Sacrifice for Sin. Therefore, S. Paul says, that "God hath set forth" the Lord Jesus Christ, "to be a propitiation through faith in His Blood, to declare His Righteousness *for the remission of Sins that are past.*"

The first truth learned by the Disciple of Christ is, therefore, that all his past sins are blotted out; that God has released him from their burden, and that their remembrance shall never be brought up against him. No word more needed than this, and none more comfortable. At the same time, if it stand alone, it is wholly inefficacious. The Death of Christ, for the pardon of sin, if considered as an isolated fact, and if wholly unconnected with any other gift or benefit, would be without value, as to the removal of Human Misery. For sin is the cause of all our calamities. Mere pardon of sin is useless, if Sin remains. There can be no salvation, deserving of that name, unless it include the eradication of the Final Root of our distresses. To announce a pardon, would be but mockery, if no change were wrought in the subjects of that amnesty.

It is therefore evident, that Salvation, although it begin with Forgiveness, cannot stop there. God must have made arrangements for an ulterior work. And so the Apostles argue, that if Christ be only *dead*, their preaching is vain, and vain also the believer's faith. And that it is of God's faithfulness and justice, not only to forgive us our sins, but also to cleanse us from all unrighteousness.

Salvation therefore divides itself into the two heads, first of Remission of Sin, and secondly of Removal of Sin. In the first respect, Man is passive: for the incompetency of the race is argued; and they cannot attain to Justification, by their own efforts. The question then might naturally arise, whether in the second respect, that passive condition was also to be maintained? Whether, as we are utterly helpless toward attaining to the Remission of our Sins, we are not equally helpless as to the process of their removal? This is the question with which the sixth chapter would appear to open.

(CHAPTER VI.)

The Doctrine of Salvation by Grace,—the Doctrine that Christ has died for our sins, and that God, for Christ's sake, forgives us, and accepts us, as sinners, and while yet ungodly,—this Doctrine can never stand alone. The Apostle has already intimated another truth, kindred and closely related to this; he has told the Romans that Christ is to Mankind for Righteousness, what Adam was to them for Sinfulness; and this is the intimation which he now developes. He shows that the State of Grace is not a merely formal condition, wherein we are affected by decrees, applicable externally but without inward power: but that there is wrought in him who, by faith, embraces the Gospel, or who is made partaker of its benefit in the way of the Lord's appointment, a spiritual change; that he is brought into vital and organic union with the Second Adam, after a manner analogous to his actual connection, by descent, with the First Adam; that by virtue of this union with the Christ, who died, was buried, and rose again, the sinner is dead unto all the past, and made alive unto another and a new spiritual existence; and that as the Dead Christ was raised from the grave unto Eternal Glory, so the dead sinner is in like manner raised from the old, fallen, and helpless condition, and restored to a healthful, vigorous, and hopeful existence. Whence it follows, that his work must be to preserve that new condition, and to keep himself from returning to the old grave whence he was taken. On his fidelity, thus far, his present and his future depend.

There is but one clue to chapter vi. Without the aid of that clue, the verses seem like a vain and vague repetition of nearly similar thoughts. With it, all becomes luminously harmonious.

This clue is, the Distinction between Nature and Character.

Human Nature is the common possession of us all. It is in all alike. But Character differs infinitely. While there is in all men but one common Nature, no two characters are precisely alike.

Nature may exist, and may be treated, apart from character. Thus an infant has human nature complete, ere yet the character be formed.

Human Nature is the subject of the operation of Divine Grace. So an infant may be regenerate by grace, while it has no character to be influenced.

But whenever God acts upon the Nature, it is in order

to reach the Character. When he acts upon the ground of this being of ours, it is in order that He may subsequently mould, form, and control all that comes up from it.

This distinction is a fundamental one, in the Apostolic writings. The Epistle to the Galatians contains it. The Epistle to the Colossians is reducible to this one idea, and is merely an expansion thereof.

So, it is constantly held in the Church. Regeneration is the invariable gift of Baptism. Renewal ought to follow. The former is a change in the Nature, and the latter in the Character.

Now the explanation of the sixth chapter is simply as follows:—The Apostle asserts the fact of a spiritual change as wrought in the Roman converts; and from the fact he argues the necessity that they should strive toward its intended end, a corresponding change in their Character. Of the change in their Nature, he speaks in the first eleven verses: it is a fact: he assumes that they know all about it: the instrument whereby it was wrought was the Sacrament of Baptism; and it is described as a mystical death unto sin and new birth unto righteousness. His language all through, on this point, is clear, plain, strong, absolute: he neither admits nor imagines any doubt on the subject: the idea of such a change is a rudimental one in the Church. Having so treated of the fact under consideration, he then passes, in verse 12, to his conclusion from it, that they ought to live according to their high and blessed state. From this point the language is not dogmatical but hortatory: it is not confident, but conveys a shade of doubtfulness. He tells them with the utmost plainness of speech, fulness, and precision, *what they have been made:* he entreats them with anxiety and fear to consider *what they ought to be.* It may be remarked that the Church follows the Apostle in this. She, in like manner, entertains and expresses no doubt as to the certain regeneration of the baptized, declaring of every child brought to the Font, that it IS, by that Sacrament, a member of Christ. But she speaks doubtfully of men in their post-baptismal state of probation: and never expresses positive and absolute assurance of the condition of the departing Soul, still recommending it to Mercy, even in the hour of death.

In these distinctions we have the clue to the chapter before us.

1. What shall we say then? Shall we continue in sin, that grace may abound?

The Apostle has spoken hitherto of the past. Now he refers to the present and the future.

"We....:" Evidently, we who have been justified and accepted; all whose past sin has been washed away.

"Shall we, ..." &c. He had said before, that the Law came in that the offence might abound, v. 20: that is to say, not in order that men might be made worse, but that in very many instances they might be convinced of sin; that its universality and its deep-rooted influence might become more conspicuous and better understood of all: and then, that the mercy of God, and His abundant gift of Grace, might be shown in all the fulness which belonged to them. The question then is: Is our present and future experience to be but a repetition of our past? or do we, once accepted, enter on a new era of existence?

"Continue...." This verb has both a transitive and an intransitive meaning: Shall we go on sinning? Shall we continue the sinful creatures that we were? Shall our deeds be the same? Shall our condition remain unaltered?

"That grace may abound?" That unlimited drafts may be made on God's Goodness. Would it be magnified thereby? Would any just praise accrue to the Lord, if He were to do nothing but perpetually absolve those who continued in sin? "In the last chapter he had spoken particularly of the abounding of grace, beyond the abounding of transgression, in that it availed through one great act of righteousness, or of justification on the part of Christ, to redeem those who had been guilty of many sins. And he had said that the very multiplication of offences, *i. e.*, of known and marked offences, by the Law, thus tended to the glory of Divine Grace. But would it be the same with transgressions committed under grace? would grace be the more glorified by their abounding? He rejects the thought with indignation. He says that this glorifying of grace through multiplied offences belongs properly to men's passing into the state of grace. It would not be real grace, if it left men to go on in sin as they did without it. The very entrance into the state of grace is by a "death unto sin," so that if we go on living in sin we are not glorifying, but contradicting it. Sins are pardoned not as continuing, but as repented of and forsaken. Grace receives us, it is true, with our infirmities upon us; but our will must renounce Sin."

2. God forbid. How shall we, that are dead to sin, live any longer therein?

The Apostle here states, with promptness and full confidence, the Spiritual Fact already mentioned: *they are dead unto sin.* And he draws his conclusion: they ought not to live any longer therein. Note, that a person, although dead unto sin, may yet go on living in it: a change may be wrought in his nature, while none has occurred in his character. The language, although figurative, expresses a spiritual reality. Every person accepted under the Gospel, in addition to the forensic act of pardon, becomes at once the subject of a Spiritual Change. The being dead unto Sin, necessarily implies the being alive unto righteousness. This change having occurred, a new set of rules, laws, and principles, apply to and bind him.

All through the Apostolic writings the distinction is observed between the Spiritual Status of Christians and their Moral and Religious Condition. The State precedes the Character. The *Life* in the Spirit is the inducement and argument to the *Walk* in the Spirit; they are not the same; they are as Cause and Effect (Gal. v. 25). So, likewise, all are called Saints, but some saints are reprobate. The Church distinguishes, accordingly, between Regeneration and Renewal: all the baptized are regenerate; but, not all the regenerate are converted.

3. Know ye not, that so many of us as were baptized into Jesus Christ were baptized into his death?

The condition of being dead to Sin is produced instrumentally by being baptized into Christ's death. This Spiritual Change occurs in Baptism. Observe, that the Apostle does not prove this: he appeals to the Romans as knowing it as well as he did: the effects of Holy Baptism constitute a rudimental branch in Christian instruction.

The expression in the preceding verse declares a condition: those in this verse state and refer to instrumentalities for producing that condition.

"Baptized into Jesus Christ:" *i. e.*, baptized into the Catholic Church, in the manner prescribed by the Lord Jesus.

"So many of us . . . . :" literally, "we, so many of us as there may be:" the statement is a universal one: all the baptized are baptized into His Death, and so dead to Sin.

"Baptized . . . . death:" Notice here, that the benefits of the Death of the Lord are conferred in Holy Baptism. In the following verse it is intimated that the benefits of His Resurrection are also conferred on us therein: and this is distinctly stated. Col. ii. 12. We see, therefore, that the Sacrament of Holy Baptism is the ordinance wherein, for the first time, the subject, duly qualified, attains to the grace and gifts which are in Christ Jesus. Those gifts have been already mentioned as three in number; 1st. Pardon; 2dly. The Germ or First Beginning of a New Life; 3dly. The Powerful Presence of the Holy Spirit. Therefore the Church, in her Creeds, has declared the "*One Baptism for the Remission of Sins;*" she affirms, in her Offices, that it is the *Sacrament of Regeneration;* and she invokes *the Holy Ghost* as then given.

4. Therefore we are buried with him by baptism into death: that like as Christ was raised up from the dead by the glory of the Father, even so we also should walk in newness of life.

The Apostle still dwells on the Fact of the Spiritual Change. He who is baptized, puts on Christ, the Second Adam, and is (after a mysterious, supernatural, and heavenly manner, which we can neither describe nor understand) united to Him, by a connection analogous to that by which he is united, by carnal descent, to the First Adam. He is baptized into Christ whole and complete; into Christ Dead, and into Christ Living; into Christ the Atoning Sacrifice, and into Christ the Exalted and Translated Conqueror; into His Death, and into His Resurrection. It is, from the instant of Baptism, the same thing as if Christ for such a man, and such a man along with Christ, had suffered, died, been buried, and risen again.

"That like as Christ, ..." &c. The object of this Spiritual Change is now stated, viz.: that a change in the Character should occur corresponding to that which has been wrought in the Nature of Man. He rose and was exalted to a heavenly inheritance; and they are baptized into Him in order that they should rise again and walk in newness of spiritual life. He left behind Him forever the Holy Sepulchre, having no more part nor lot therein; and so ought they, having been delivered from the grave of a former sinful condition, to return to their old sins no more. And the Apostle assigns this newness of life, as the result had in view when we were baptized.

"By the Glory of the Father:" the Glory of that Divine Life, incorruptible and powerful, by which, both Christ was raised up, and we also are restored to newness of life, and made like unto God.

It is of the highest necessity, that all the statements respecting the benefits of Holy Baptism, as made by S. Paul, should be cast together, and so regarded at one view. See, then, this passage, where we are said to be buried with Him, by Baptism, into death: See Col. ii. 12, where we are said to be risen with Him also therein, and where the faith required of him who desires to receive that Holy Sacrament is a faith in the Power of God as the Raiser-from-Death: See, also, Ephes. i. 19, where it is said that the Power of God to *us*, is the same which He wrought when He raised up *Christ* from death: See, also, Gal. iii. 27, where he says that as many as have been baptized into Christ have put on Christ; and 2 Cor. v. 17, where it is said that they who are in Christ are new creatures: also Titus iii. 5, where, stating that our salvation is not of works but of grace, he makes mention, first, in order of its application to us, of the "washing of regeneration:" and couples it with the renewing of the Holy Ghost: also Col. iii. and iv. chapters, *passim*, in which every duty of the Christian Life is based upon the antecedent fact of a new relationship to God founded in Holy Baptism: also Eph. v. 25, 26, where the sanctifying and cleansing of the Church is spoken of in connection with the instrumentality of "the washing of water:" also Rom. vi. 6, compared with Ephes. iv. 21, 22, 23, 24, where we are taught, that in Baptism it is the "old man" which is crucified and dead with Christ," and that the "new man," which takes its place, is *created* (cf. again 2 Cor. v. 17) in righteousness and true holiness.

Now it should seem impossible to examine these statements without becoming convinced, 1st, that the Gift and Grace of the Gospel are first communicated in Baptism, as an Instrumental Cause or Means; and 2dly, that Forgiveness of Sin forms but a part of the entire Gospel Benefit. The Forgiveness of Sin is but a preliminary step toward something far greater: if we are buried with Christ, it is but for a moment, to the end that we may rise and live with Him forever. And one must also perceive that all this language would be but mockery, unless God Almighty had in contemplation, and had begun to effect, in Christ, a complete purifying and renewal of the mass of Humanity. That He should leave men in their old condition, and yet address them, by His Apostles, in language like this, would be inexplicable. The Apostolic writings do not indeed contain any full development or scientific treatment of this mighty theme; but a knowledge of it is presupposed in the persons addressed; and rightly so, for it seems to have been the leading idea of that grand System of Christianity, which has for its objects, the Remission of the Sinfulness of Man and its Ultimate Removal. It is essential, moreover, to the right understanding of the subject, that we carefully distinguish between the Spiritual Change, the Instrument whereby it is effected, and the Ultimate End. He who accepts the Gospel is, by Baptism, as an Instrument, made dead unto sin and alive unto righteousness, this being a spiritual change, in the nature, not in the character. It is then his duty to co-operate with the Grace of God, until his moral character be completely changed, and until he grow to the likeness of the Lord Jesus. In this chapter of the Epistle to the Romans, the Apostle assumes, as a fact rudimental in Christianity, the change under question; and he argues thence as to the duties of the converts. His language is adapted precisely to this difference: he speaks boldly, absolutely, of their being dead to sin; but doubtfully and anxiously of their living in Grace. In the one case, he says, ye ARE; in the other, ye SHOULD BE. And this analogy is followed by the Church: she speaks, with absolute certainty, of every duly baptized person, as regenerate: she speaks, with the greatest caution and reserve, of those who are in post-baptismal probation: she never speaks with positive and absolute assurance of the departed. The *State* is a fact: the use we make of our advantages is doubtful.

The distinction between Nature and Character is the clue to this chapter. In the first eleven verses he speaks, absolutely, of the state of the Romans as dead to sin and alive unto GOD. At the 12th verse he changes his style, and exhorts them not to fall back into the slough whence they were drawn.

5. For if we have been planted together in the likeness of his death, we shall be also

The language is figurative, and taken from the floral or vegetable kingdom; but vastly more than figurative language, in this, that it expresses a

in the likeness of *his* resurrection:

spiritual reality. The figures used by our Lord, and repeated by His Apostles, are not mere empty tropes, but living signs of correspondent truths in the Mystical Sphere of Redemption, *e. g.*, the Apostle is here only adopting the expressions first used by the Lord (see S. John xv. 1–8), in discourse to His Disciples; and that discourse of our Lord's is truly expressive of real and actual, though supernatural and incomprehensible union between Himself and His people. A man is said to be *in* Christ: he is bidden to abide in Him: he is warned of the danger and consequence of not abiding in Him. This is our Lord's own language. The connected ideas, 1st, that all who are baptized into Christ are *in* Him; and 2dly, that all who are in Him are new creatures: these are the Apostolic amplification of the Lord's words.

"If" is not hypothetical: it means "since," as in Col. iii. 1.

"Planted together in the likeness of His Death." All the power of spiritual life and growth is in Christ; and this is conferred upon us in the Holy Sacrament. The phrase means the same as planted together with Him in Baptism: grafted into Him in that rite which affords a likeness of His Death, by our descent into the wave, and of His Resurrection by our emerging therefrom.

6. Knowing this, that our old man is crucified with *him*, that the body of sin might be destroyed, that henceforth we should not serve sin.

It might be thought that the penitential discipline of the Christian is here referred to. But on reflection, the decision is against such a view. In this and verse 7, Christ seems to be spoken of. "Our old Man," is the Nature which He assumed; it was crucified on His Cross; as the Body of Sin, *i. e.*, a Body subject to the consequences of Sin, it was destroyed, and that Body of Death lives no longer. But in place of it there is come the Glorified and Immortal Body of the Risen Christ. And all this was done, in order that they, who share in the infirmities and distresses to which the Ancient Body of Death is subject, and from which it was delivered through Christ, may likewise be delivered from Bondage to Sin and Death.

The verses, 6–13, may thus be freely paraphrased:

6. It was our "old man" which the Lord assumed;

a frail, imperfect, weak, and mortal nature, capable of suffering, and liable to die. That "old man" was crucified, in the Person of the Son of God, on Calvary. That "body of sin" (that nature subject to temptation, sorrow, and the assaults of the Devil, that body which "was made sin for us,") was thus destroyed, in accordance with the general law of death. And out of it there came the Body of Life, and Glory, and Immortal Power. This was done, that all who have the like nature, might be rescued similarly from the service of sin.
7. For he that is dead is freed from sin: the old body
of sin is now dead in Christ, and sin and death
8. have no more power of it. Therefore we, who are
9, 10. dead unto sin, and freed from it in Christ, have
the future prospect of glory assured to us by the
11. mystery of His Resurrection; and are certain of
our union with Him in the Death and in the Life
12, 13. alike. Out of this assurance grows the new law of
our life.

7. For he that is dead is freed from sin.

Christ is still referred to. He, who bore our "old man," in His Body, on the tree, was freed from the power of Death and Hell by His Sacrifice. We likewise are freed from sin, *i. e.*, from its dominion, as being dead in Him; for all who are dead to sin are free from its power.

8. Now if we be dead with Christ, we believe that we shall also live with him:

9. Knowing that Christ being raised from the dead dieth no more; death hath no more dominion over him.

10. For in that he died, he died unto sin once: but in that he liveth, he liveth unto God.

11. Likewise reckon ye also yourselves to be dead indeed unto sin, but alive unto God through Jesus Christ our Lord.

The spiritual change has a future reference: it looks to a glorious immortality, after the fashion of our Lord's Resurrection.

Knowing, as they did, all the story concerning the Lord; His glorious triumph over death, and His exalted Life in Heaven; all which was, in fact, the glorifying and exalting of this nature of ours.

11. The Apostle reaffirms, in the same positive, unqualified, and absolute way as before, the spiritual fact of which mention has been made. A wonderful Change had passed on them. They should "reckon themselves," *i. e.*, be perfectly certain that

they are, "indeed," in very truth, "dead unto Sin, and alive unto God."

12. Let not sin therefore reign in your mortal body, that ye should obey it in the lusts thereof.

13. Neither yield ye your members *as* instruments of unrighteousness unto sin: but yield yourselves unto God, as those that are alive from the dead, and your members *as* instruments of righteousness unto God.

14. For sin shall not have dominion over you: for ye are not under the law, but under grace.

12. The Hortatory part now begins: here is a transition. Note the bearing of verses 11 and 12 on each other. *Because* they are dead unto sin, &c., *therefore* they must not permit sin to reign over them. Later systems of theology reverse this order; they would say, because men live righteously, therefore they are dead to sin; because they are converted, therefore are they born again. But these are "other gospels," not the old one.

The Apostle has said thus far that sin OUGHT not to reign over us and to hold us in subjection. He now adds that it SHALL not. There appears to be a logical sequence in these two thoughts, or rather in these two methods of presenting the subject.

For if God Almighty lays upon us any injunction, we infer that we must possess, through Him, the power of fulfilling it. So that the duty of being free from the bondage of Sin implies the possibility of being so; we must be able to keep in that liberty wherewith Christ hath made us free.

And in another point of view this assurance is needed. For after our being accepted with God, we still commit many transgressions. Should not the continued presence of Sin lead us to despair? Must we not count ourselves alienated from God? By no means. For we are not now under the Law, but under Grace. God requires of us, not the bond-service of slaves, but the loving obedience of children.

14. The last words in verse 13 suggest a thought which the Apostle carries out: for verse 19 is almost word for word a repetition of verse 13. The intermediate verses form a kind of parenthesis, they develope the general thought, but add no new idea. In verse 13 he had said, ye should not be, ye ought not to be, the servants of Sin: ye ought to be the servants of God. From this it is clear that a choice still remains with the regenerate: they may go back to the service of Sin. Therefore the word "for," with which verse 14 begins, should be taken as having a conditional

character. "For," if ye will but yield yourselves unreservedly to God, "sin shall not have dominion over you." And why? Because ye are not under the Law, but under Grace.

It is this idea of being under Grace and not under the Law, which the Apostle fully developes in the third part of Section III. In the comment on that Section it will receive the full treatment which it requires.

15. What then? shall we sin, because we are not under the law, but under grace? God forbid.

A repetition of the question in the 1st verse of this chapter. Great is the peril of abusing the Doctrine of Salvation by Grace. Note, that the Apostle gives a slight variation to the answer. He had asked, Shall we wilfully continue in sin? and he answered, No; because we are dead to it in Christ. Now, asking the same question, he replies, No; because we are become the servants of God.

16. Know ye not, that to whom ye yield yourselves servants to obey, his servants ye are to whom ye obey; whether of sin unto death, or of obedience unto righteousness?

17. But God be thanked, that ye were the servants of sin, but ye have obeyed from the heart that form of doctrine which was delivered you.

18. Being then made free from sin, ye became the servants of righteousness.

19. I speak after the manner of men because of the infirmity of your flesh: for as ye have yielded your members servants to uncleanness and to iniquity unto iniquity; even so now yield your members servants to righteousness unto holiness.

20. For when ye were

The allegory, if it may so be called, of the two services, is here employed: a familiar illustration. He contrasts the Service of Sin and that of God; compares the masters, the duty, and the wages.

A Greek idiom, in verse 17. To Anglicize it, understand "although" between "that" and "ye," and suppress "but." God be thanked that ye were brought out of the old bondage to sin.

"Form of Doctrine...." Probably the Creed of the Church is referred to.

"From the heart...." They had fully and cordially received the Church System with all which it implies.

18. They were not set absolutely free: they did but enter another service.

19. A repetition of the thought in verse 13. Ye must be the faithful and true servants of Righteousness.

20. When given up to the service of sin, ye felt no sense of restraint and no obligations elsewhere: and so ye were

the servants of sin, ye were free from righteousness.

21. What fruit had ye then in those things whereof ye are now ashamed? for the end of those things *is* death.

22. But now being made free from sin, and become servants to God, ye have your fruit unto holiness, and the end everlasting life.

23. For the wages of sin *is* death; but the gift of God *is* eternal life through Jesus Christ our Lord.

able to form a correct idea what that service was worth.

A challenge to them, to say, frankly, what a sinful career comes to in respect of reward. Understand, after the interrogation, "None:" and then go on, "for the end," &c.

A contrast of the service of God and that of Sin. Holiness is its fruit: that is to say, holiness is the duty, a work which the servant is expected to render.

"Wages of Sin." . . . . "Gift of God." . . . . Note, that the phraseology changes: he does not say, "Wages of God;" such a term would be singularly inappropriate; for our Salvation is of Grace, and not at all of debt.

METHOD AND MEANS OF SALVATION.

Part 3d. The Work of the Holy Ghost unto Righteousness.

The seventh and eighth chapters of the Epistle should be read together: the subject is continuous, and the closing and opening verses (vii. 25; viii. 1) should have no break between them.

The Apostle addresses himself particularly to such as, by direct revelation, know, in its full excellence and beauty, the Moral Law of God.

He considers the case of fallen Man as it stands in relation to that Law: and he presents a moving picture of the anguish and miseries wherein the Sinner is bound, through inability to fulfil that Law, and of the method of his deliverance, under the Gospel, from that incompetent and most unhappy condition.

Before passing to the commentary on the text, several points must be clearly understood and retained in mind:

1st. The Law here spoken of, cannot be the Jewish Ceremonial or Ritual System; for on this supposition we could not account for the breadth and general applicability of the expressions. It is the Moral Law of God; that Law, in whatever way made known to men, whether through the conscience and the heart; or, as on Mount Sinai, in written characters; or, as when our Lord Jesus Christ repeated it, by the living Preacher of truth.

2dly. The person described as passing through the Spiritual struggle herein recounted, is not the Apostle himself (as though, like one in a modern prayer-meeting, he were giving his "experience"); still less can the Christian be considered as the subject. But the case supposed is that of THE SINNER in general; of the Soul for which Christ died: and, although the Holy Apostle uses the first person (verses 9 to 25 inclusive), yet is this but a very common and well-known figure of animated speech. The person, the character described is the Sinner, as he passes out of a fallen and lost condition, into one of Grace and Salvation.

3dly. "Sin," must be here understood, not as Actual, but as Original; the old fault and corruption of the Nature of every one descended from Adam. This is represented as resident in the Flesh; in the Body, and in its members; and its presence there occasions and constitutes "the Law of Sin and Death." To the motions of this Law of Sin and Death, all the misery of man is due. There are certain relations, original and necessary, between the Law of God and the Soul; but these are disturbed and deranged by the existence and power of this "Law in the Members;" and thus it results that the Law of God, which should be ever the joy and delight of the Soul, becomes for it a terror. There is a conflict between the Soul, desiring the Law of God, and the Flesh, ruled over by the Law of Sin; and, in this distracted state, Man is reduced to extremity and brought face to face with death. No change has occurred, meanwhile, in the Law of God; but the change is in him and in his relations to it; and this is due to the power of Sin within his flesh.

4thly. Therefore, and as a consequence, the "being dead to the Law," cannot mean the ceasing to have relations to it, the being made independent of it, the being no longer held and bound to obey it; for that were impossible. The relations between the Moral Law of God and Man are just as necessary as those between the Planets and the influences which keep them in their orbit, or those between the particles of matter and the attraction of Gravitation. But it is the being dead to it, in respect to those new relations which it has assumed toward Man as a Sinner. And, because those relations arise from the presence of the new, foreign, and exotic principle of Sinfulness, and from its efficiency through the Law of Sin and Death—therefore the "being dead unto the Law" can result only from an attack upon that foreign principle itself, at its inmost seats, and through the destruction of that unnatural Law. These being affected or destroyed, the original relations between the Law of God and the Soul of Man are re-established, and his deliverance is complete. But this change and deliverance are effected through the Gospel, wherein we are dead unto Sinfulness and alive unto God; freed, that is, from the condemnation of Guilt, and invested with the power of fulfilling all acceptable Righteousness, through the gift and transforming presence of the Holy Ghost.

Having thus explained the meaning of the leading terms of this part of the Section, let us try to take, at the outset, a comprehensive view of the Apostle's argument. He speaks, throughout, of the Law of God in its relation to the Sinner. First, then, of Law in general:

Law is a Rule of Action.

The Laws of God are rules drawn from, or founded upon the Facts of His own Being, and imposed by Him upon His creatures.

But God has made each of His creatures for some definite end, and has adapted the nature of each to its end.

The Laws of God may be considered as expressions of His will concerning His creatures, and as descriptive of the design and intention of their being. Every Law is proportioned to the capacity of the subject on whom it is imposed, and refers to those characteristics, powers, and faculties which form its essential and distinctive nature.

As there are various kinds of creatures, so are there various Laws.

The Moral Law is that one, among these various Laws, which contains the Rule of Action for Man, as a Moral Agent, and as a Living Soul.

This Moral Law is a Rule drawn from the facts of God's Being; adapted to the nature of Man; and imposed on him for the regulation of all his thoughts, words and deeds.

It is founded on these principles: that the perfection of Humanity consists in likeness to God; that the happiness of Men must consist in union with God; and that there cannot be union where there is not Similarity.

Its substance is in brief: that Man, in order to be useful and happy, must love his Creator and do His will.

The Moral Law of God is wholly incapable of alteration, or abrogation. It is simply the rule of a being coming from God, and dependent upon Him; and while that being continues to exist, this Law must be as natural and necessary to it, as an atmosphere to the lungs.

The Moral Law of God, is, then, the simple expression of the facts of our relationship to the Almighty; and it contains the method and manner of that life which men ought to lead, as His creatures, and, by leading which, they should never be separated from Him.

But we have to consider the change which comes on Man through transgression. Through one Man Sinfulness entered into the world, and Death by Sin.

The Sinner, not being yet utterly lost and gone from hope, but being, and having been retained, through the mercy of God, in a condition in which Salvation is possible for him, still knows and reverences the Moral Law. As the law of his better self, he loves and delights in it: and he would fain fulfil it, and live thereby. He knows that if he could fulfil it, he should live.

But Sinfulness exists, in his body, in his members, and in his flesh. This causes a moral disorder: and the desire of his heart toward the Holy Law and the better life, is thwarted and left utterly helpless, as respects realization.

The Sinner perceives without, a Pure, Holy, and Good Rule of Life, which he knows to express the order of his true existence, and in obedience to which, his happiness should be secured. At the same time he finds, within, a merciless and exacting tyranny which binds him fast, and keeps him away from the path of life.

The more clearly the Higher Law is known, the more desperate his condition becomes. If he did not know the Law at all, he would feel himself far less guilty. It is through knowledge thereof that he perceives himself to be as dead.

The Law, thus known to him, can neither justify nor sanctify him. It is the revelation to him of that Perfect

Purity, Holiness, and Excellence from which he is hopelessly removed. It is the manifestation to him of all that he ought to be. But it brings him no nearer to God.

The cause of this wretched state is his Sinfulness. Its effect is twofold: 1st, to ruin all his present, and, 2dly, to make him despair for all his past. He cannot live as he ought: and he cannot make amends for the days that are gone. Thus is he bound, hand and foot, and delivered over unto death.

Meanwhile, the Moral Law changes its relation to him. For the unfallen and sinless creature, who lives according to its terms, it is a delight and a joy: since the consciousness that one is doing what he ought, and doing it well, must give endless contentment. But that same Law, as contemplated by the fallen and lost wretch, becomes to him a Prophet of Vengeance and a Harbinger of Despair: for it stands above him, calm and inexorable, unchanging and unmoved, a Nemesis of Tribulation and Wrath. In it there can be no change . . . . and, since he is what he is, what shall the end be? . . . .

Such is the desperate and inextricable condition of the Sinner: and such is the aspect of the mortal struggle of the Soul.

Who shall deliver him from that state?

None but Jesus Christ, through His Gospel.

How is that deliverance effected?

By the introduction of another Element into the problem, the Law of the Spirit of Life in Christ Jesus.

The Moral Law is not destroyed, nor abrogated, nor weakened, in anywise.

And the Law of Sin and Death which is in the members, is not altogether taken away: for the old infection of the nature yet remains even in the regenerate.

But a principle of Spiritual Life is introduced into the nature; and the power whereby the Lord Jesus was raised up from the dead, is engaged for the complete deliverance of the Sinner, both in soul and in body, from the bondage and thraldom of his fallen and lost condition.

He is assured of full pardon for the past; he is declared to be dead to the Law of Sin in his members; he is enabled to obey the true law of his being; he is assured of acceptance in respect of his sincerity. To the Moral Law, so far as it formerly prophesied to him of judgment and wrath, he is dead; and it, as a messenger of vengeance, is dead to him. It revives to him, and he revives to it, as the blessed Rule of Life: this is because the Lord Jesus has purchased indulgence, in respect to all his *quasi*-involuntary infractions thereof, and has obtained for him the power of fulfilling it through the Holy Spirit. To the Law of Sin and Death, he is dead; as knowing that Christ being risen from the dead dieth no more, and that they that are Christ's are made partakers of His Resurrection. The Law of the Spirit of Life in Christ Jesus, teaches him these things: it assures him that God loves the world, and accepts the love of the convert in lieu of perfect obedience: and thus all the sorrow terminates, and ends in the grand principle that Love is the fulfilling of the Law.

"Sin is the transgression of the Law:"

But, "Love is the fulfilling of the Law."

Thus the Almighty, under the Gospel, balances, not Sin against Perfect Obedience, but Sin against Love. He who will truly love God and the Lord Jesus Christ, shall be counted as dead unto Sin: and for the heart of simple love, Sin, and Death, and the threatenings of the Law, have no more terror.

This Love is commended to us, 1st, by the Mission of God's Only Begotten Son; and, 2dly, by our adoption, for Christ's sake, to be God's children. (14–17.)

For this manifestation, all the world has been waiting, through long and weary ages of trouble. (18–27.)

But now, under the Gospel, the blessed Mystery is fully revealed, and all works together for the triumph of Love. (28–30.)

Wherefore the Apostle concludes with his soul-thrilling anthem of praise, and magnifies the Love of Christ, glorying and rejoicing in it forever. (31–39.)

(CHAPTER VII.)

1. Know ye not, brethren, (for I speak to them that know the law,) how that the law hath dominion over a man as long as he liveth?

"The Law....:" not the ceremonial law of the Jews, nor yet the Mosaic law in general, but the Moral Law of God, in that high and full sense explained in the introductory remarks.

"I speak," &c. He addresses such as have a knowledge of that Law; of its bearings upon us, of the joy and the difficulty of obeying it.

"Hath dominion." The context, and the drift of the thought, imply an arbitrary and severe dominion, and one under which the man is in a reluctant bondage. But these relations between the Law and Man are due to sinfulness: therefore, Man is here referred to as not yet under grace; and, "as long as he liveth," signifies, as long as he continues in his natural condition, unaided and unrelieved by the Gospel Gift.

It is to be especially noted, at the outset, and borne in mind all through the discussion, that to Man, unfallen, the Law of God presents no terrors, but is sweet and precious, holy and good, so that he may say, "Lord, what love have I unto Thy Law! all the day long is my study in it; Thy Law do I love; it is sweeter than honey unto my mouth," &c., &c. But, to fallen and guilty Man, without the knowledge of God's Grace, the Law assumes another form, and becomes a terror; it ceases to be a friendly guide, and becomes an arbitrary Master; it hath dominion over him, as long as he remains unabsolved and unrenewed. The change is not in the Law, but in him. These unhappy relations are not original nor natural; but secondary, and novel. They result from the presence of sin. They are remedied by the Gospel Gift; and the old and happy relations of Man to the Law are restored thereby.

2. For the woman which hath an husband is bound by the law to *her* husband so long as he liveth; but if the husband be dead, she is loosed from the law of *her* husband.
3. So then if, while *her* husband liveth, she be married to another man, she shall be called an adulteress: but if her husband be dead, she is free from that law; so that she is no adulteress, though she be married to another man.
4. Wherefore, my brethren, ye also are

An illustration is taken from the marriage relation. As the wife is bound to her husband, so is the Soul to its Master, the Law.

"The law of her husband . . . . :" *i. e.*, the law which binds her to her husband.

"Called an adulteress . . . . :" In Scripture usage, *to be called* aught is *to be* that which one is called: it is a sacred idiom, as one might say, and universal, or nearly so.

4. "Dead to the Law. . . . :" Not as having no farther relationship to it, or obligation to fulfil it: for that were impossible; the Law of Human Nature being as fixed and unchangeable as Human Nature itself. But dead, as to the relationships which exist be-

become dead to the law by the body of Christ; that ye should be married to another, *even* to him who is raised from the dead, that we should bring forth fruit unto God.

tween that Pure and Perfect Law of God and the lost and ruined soul: dead to the Law regarded as a Task-master and a Tyrant; dead to the Law inasmuch as it is become to the sinner a Prophet of Evil and a Boder of Damnation: dead to it, as sinful, but alive unto it as justified (for see the last words, "that we should bring forth fruit unto God").

"Ye . . . . :" Ye who are in Christ Jesus; ye who have been buried with Him in Baptism, and who are raised with Him therein.

"By the Body of Christ . . . . :" The human Body of the Lord, which was offered upon the Cross as a Sacrifice for Sin, and was raised again from death to be a head and fountain of Grace. The propriety of this reference to Christ's Body is seen, when we consider that in the body, the members, and the flesh, of the sinner is the especial and original seat of sinfulness. So Bengel: "*Per corpus:* magnum mysterium. Cur in expiatione peccati mentio fit plerumque Corporis Christi præ Anima? Resp. Peccati theatrum et officina caro nostra est: huic medetur Sancta Caro Filii Dei."

"Married to another . . . . :" *i. e.*, to our Lord Jesus Christ. Compare the words of the Apostle, Ephes. v. 23–32, and 2 Cor. xi. 2. The Sacrament of Matrimony is the living type of the union between God and the Soul, between Christ and the Church. The Old Testament prophets represent the transgressions of Israel and Judah under the figure of adultery and whoredom; the type is an ancient one.

"That we should bring," &c.: Hence it is evident that the being dead to the Law is not the being released from the duty to fulfil righteousness; for Christ rose again in order that He might purchase for us, and confer upon us, the power of Holy Obedience.

5. For when we were in the flesh, the motions of sins, which were by the law, did work in our members to bring forth fruit unto death.

"In the flesh . . . . :" in our natural condition; before the Grace of the Gospel had been received.

"The motions of sins . . . . :" the uneasy movements of the original Root and Spring of Moral Depravity.

"Which were by the Law . . . . :" which were known

and recognized as sins, by means of the convictions produced by the Law: a thought which is presently developed at greater length.

"In our members . . . . :" In the flesh is the seat of Sinfulness and Death.

6. But now we are delivered from the law, that being dead wherein we were held; that we should serve in newness of spirit, and not *in* the oldness of the letter.

"Delivered, &c. . . . . :" an expression equivalent to that previous one of being dead thereto.

"That being dead . . . . :" This is not probably the true reading: in the Greek, as established by the best authorities, it is, not ἀποθανόντος, but ἀποθανόντες, and the verse should have been translated, "but now, being dead, we are freed from the Law in which we were held." To say, that the Law is dead, would not be literally true, and could only be tolerated as a very strong figure.

"The letter . . . . :" The Letter, is not the Law considered by itself, since it is a spiritual and a live thing (cf. verse 14, and Acts vii. 38). But it is the Law considered with reference to the sinner, to whom it cannot give spirit and life, but leaves him helpless. Our service is not to be as of old, as to a rigid and inflexible Master whom we could never hope to satisfy: but it is a new service, and rendered by us as renewed by the Spirit of God.

7. What shall we say then? *Is* the law sin? God forbid. Nay, I had not known sin, but by the law: for I had not known lust, except the

The objection raised in this verse is by no means an unnatural one: for it has been said, that we are "dead to the Law," and "delivered from the Law," and especially that the sins, whose motions wrought in our members unto death, were by the Law. Hence, one might fall into the error of supposing that the Law was somehow a cause of Sin, and that the blame should fall upon it, and not upon the Sinner.

"Is the Law sin?" The question is at once answered in the negative. The Law is not the cause of Sin; nor is it responsible in any way for our calamities and distresses.

"I had not known . . . . :" The Apostle here adopts the 1st person, with indefinite reference, for the sake of perspicuity, and as giving animation to the style.

"I had not known Sin, &c. . . . . :" Sinfulness is latent in the members and in the being. Were the Law of God entirely unknown, the existence of Sinfulness in our acts would of course remain equally unknown. It is the knowledge which we enjoy of the Perfect Law of God, which shows us our perversity and depravity: and the more clearly we comprehend the marvellous excellence of that Rule of Holy Action, the more fully must we perceive our own shocking condition.

law had said, Thou shalt not covet.
8. But sin, taking occasion by the commandment, wrought in me all manner of concupiscence. For without the law sin *was* dead.

"Thou shalt not covet . . . .:" Unwilling to refer to the heaviest kinds of crimes, or perhaps thinking it more practical to select some very widely prevalent sin by way of illustration, the Apostle chooses for that purpose the 10th Commandment. The thought is, that one might not know an act to be sinful, unless he had ascertained that it was forbidden: "I had not known lust" to be evil. Men would have committed Sin, but they would not have known the nature of it. Sin is Sin, whatever our view of it may be: but the lower men stand in the scale of enlightenment, the less they feel its enormity.

8. Sin . . . .:" *i. e.*, Sinfulness; the primal and inherent evil and taint of the Nature of Mankind.

"Taking occasion . . . .:" *i. e.*, finding a favourable opportunity against us: Sinfulness is here personified as an Agent hostile to human peace.

"By the Commandment, ...:" *i. e.*, by the Law, as becoming more clearly known.

"Wrought . . . concupiscence . . . .:" The analysis is a simple one: when the laws of God become known, we at once begin to perceive our state of opposition to them; we think of every evil motion of our hearts as a sin; we feel as sins, what we may not have so regarded previously; we feel condemned before God for such acts; we pass to a sensation of discouragement, as if there were no use in trying to be good, because we cannot wholly rid ourselves of evil; and thence it may come to a kind of perverse and froward resolve to continue in Sin and get what good of it we can. The mere fact that a thing is forbidden, may set a man to desire it: the warning against evil, may tempt some one to commit it, who otherwise would have been comparatively indifferent. To forbid the flesh its pleas ures and indulgences, is to rouse up a spirit of resistance and wilfulness, and to excite stronger desire.

"Without the Law Sin was dead." Translate, "is dead." The proposition is absolutely true. Cf. iv. 15; v. 13., "Without the Law;" *i. e.*, without a knowledge of the Law, on the part of men; "Sin is dead," *i. e.*, there can be no convictions of Sinfulness, and it can have no power at all to torment and afflict the conscience and mind. Sin cannot declare itself, where the Moral Law of God is unknown: but it must, of course, exist, the same. The whole language relates to the subjective condition of the mind, in its apprehension of the real nature of Sin, and the punishment thereof. The whole thought is intensely and exclusively subjective.

9. For I was alive without the law once: but when the commandment came, sin revived, and I died.

"I was alive . . . .:" *i. e.*, in my own eyes; I thought that it was well with me; I seemed to myself to live and to be safe.

"Without the Law . . . .:" *i. e.*, before coming to the full knowledge of God's Will and Commandments.

"Came, ...:" *i. e.*, came to my knowledge.

"Sin revived . . . .:" Sinfulness, that evil agent, clenched me at once: and "I died;" *i. e.*, I perceived myself to be a lost and dying wretch.

10. And the commandment, which *was ordained* to life, I found *to be* unto death.

"The Commandment . . . .:" the Moral Law as already explained.

"Which was to life . . . .:" for that Law contains the rule of life, and is the perfect guide of Man, considered as a spiritual and immortal being.

"Unto death . . . .:" In its effects; for the sinner cannot obey it; and, therefore, humanly speaking, must die.

11. For sin, taking occasion by the commandment, deceived me, and by it slew *me*.

11. "For Sin . . . .:" not the Law. but Sinfulness: it slew him, on occasion of the knowledge of the Law. It is not *the Law* which is the cause of death, but Sin: the Law is an occasion only.

"Deceived me . . . .:" Led me into devious and interminable ways, as the murderer leads the traveller far off from help: led me unawares, until, not knowing whither I went, I fell into the ways of death.

12. Wherefore the

Full response is made to the ques-

law *is* holy, and the commandment holy, and just, and good.

tion raised in verse 7. These expressions of the holy Apostle deserve to be weighed in connection with the wild blasphemies of the Antinomian Scheme, as well as by all who would separate the Faith and the Righteousness of the Gospel. The account of the Moral Law as here given, is forever its just and correct description. It is natural to Man to reverence, to delight in, and to love that Law; and there can be no opposition between its requirements and our happiness and peace, unless we, by our offences, give rise to such opposition. See the 119th Psalm, for a full devotional exposition of this thought: it is a long act of prayer and holy desire toward the Law of God, with search to know how to fulfil it.

13. Was then that which is good made death unto me? God forbid. But sin, that it might appear sin, working death in me by that which is good; that sin by the commandment might become exceeding sinful.

The idea that the Law of God can be in itself a cause or source of death to men, is preposterous and contradictory: for the Law is simply the expression of God's will concerning us, that we should be holy as He is holy, and so should be happy in and with Him. Sinfulness distorts all our relations to that "holy, just, and good" Commandment. Sin, availing itself of that blessed standard, as a means of bringing the Sinner to confusion, leads him to count himself as utterly lost and dead, and cuts him off from that perfect path of life, and even from the effort to keep it. And thus, through the Commandment, as perverted to its diabolical purpose, Sin grows to be an intolerable oppressor, and reduces its victim to despair, between his knowledge of the Law and desire toward it, and his obstinate and perverse craving for the pleasures of Sin. That struggle the Apostle now proceeds to describe. And the transition is not an unnatural one just here: for it is of the nature of all usurpations, that a reaction finally takes place when the burden becomes too intolerable. Sin, when become exceeding sinful, when felt in all the weight of its power, and with all its miserable consequences, compels the sufferer to cast about for some way of escape, if any such there be. (A literal rendering of this somewhat complicated passage, would be as follows:—"Was then the good (Law) the cause of my ruin? Certainly not: but Sin (was the cause of it), which, 'that it might appear Sin,' in other words, to show (or showing) its character, wrought ruin by means of the good (Law), thus displaying its detestable nature.")

14. For we know that the law is spiritual: but I am carnal, sold under sin.

These are the two convictions which destroy the peace of the soul. The knowledge that the Moral Law of God is the spiritual rule of life: and the knowledge that the sinner is bound fast, so as to be unable to walk thereafter.

15. For that which I do I allow not: for what I would, that do I not; but what I hate, that do I.

This is the proof of what has just been said. "For," refers to the words next preceding: "I may indeed say of myself that I am sold under sin, because," &c. He describes the bondage, not as exculpating himself, but as accusing the tyranny of Sin, and as deploring his wretched state.

On the use of the pronoun of the first person, see the introductory observations on this Section.

"I allow not." The Greek word signifies "I know not:" as if he said, I know not the real character, the end, the results of what I do. Or else the word may be taken in the sense of "I like not, I do not approve of."

"That which I do . . . . that do I . . . .:" both refer to the sins of the person described.

"What I would . . . .:" To wit, works of holiness, goodness, excellence. The human mind, so far as it may be called by that name, and has not become quite fiendish, has in it some reverence for Goodness, and some desire, more or less strong, to be good. The greatest sinners have left testimony of their secret reverence for Sanctity and Virtue. The love of these qualities is innate, and we never entirely lose it.

16. If then I do that which I would not, I consent unto the law that *it is* good.
17. Now then it is no more I that do it, but sin that dwelleth in me.

The Apostle would argue, that from the contradiction thus described between desire and action, two conclusions must logically and of necessity follow:

(*a*) The sinner becomes a witness to the purity and goodness of the law:

(*b*) He is the sufficient evidence that it is not so much the real and proper man who does all the evil, but that it must be ascribed to the Law of Sin and Death in his members.

The Law of God is vindicated on the one hand: the honour of Humanity is saved on the other.

18. For I know that in me (that is, in my flesh,) dwelleth no good thing: for to will is present with me; but *how* to perform that which is good I find not.

19. For the good that I would I do not: but the evil which I would not, that I do.

20. Now if I do that I would not, it is no more I that do it, but sin that dwelleth in me.

As the words with which verse 17 closes are repeated in verse 20, these three verses would seem to be intended as a proof of the position advanced, that it is not Man himself, not the "I," the "Ego," but the Sinfulness within him which thus works ruin upon him.

18. "In me:" The Sinner, in his natural condition, is meant.

"Flesh:" The Seat of the Law of Sin and Death is the mortal and corruptible body.

20. "It is no more I that do it:" The real man is represented by, and resides especially in, the Reason and the Conscience: these form the better part of the man. And yet they are enslaved to Sin; and so the whole being is domineered over and subdued.

21. I find then a law, that, when I would do good, evil is present with me.

22. For I delight in the law of God after the inward man:

21. "A law . . . .:" The same which is presently called the law of Sin and Death.

22. "Inward man . . . .:" The soul; the spiritual part; the Reason, Conscience, and Affections: no reference to the soul considered as renewed by the Grace of God: it means, the soul and spirit as they were left by the Fall, and before receiving Divine Grace.

"I delight in the Law of God . . . .:" Cf. Psalm xix. 7–11. The mind naturally loves and delights in the Law of God: it would argue a complete and hopeless apostasy, if this were not true of the race in general. This feeling is the first and natural rule of the being. But there has intruded itself within us another and a foreign and alien principle of evil, and its presence produces utter discord. There are two laws within us, warring against each other, and causing an intolerable condition of misery and wretchedness.

23. But I see another law in my members, warring against the law of my mind, and bringing me into captivity to the law of sin which is in my members.

It must be noted, on this verse, that the Apostle distinguishes between the "law of sin," and "another law," as he terms it: and that, in like manner, he distinguishes in the context, between the "Law of God," and the "law of the mind:" and that presently he speaks of the "law of the Spirit of Life in Christ Jesus." The present, therefore, seems to be the suitable place, for speaking generally of these divers "laws" here mentioned, and of explaining the distinctions which seem to exist among them.

Five times, and in five different ways, is this term used: for we read of these following "laws:"

(A) The Law of God . . . . (verse 22).

(*a*) The Law of the Mind . . . . (verse 23).

(B) The Law of Sin . . . . (verse 23).

(*b*) Another law in the members, not named . . . . (verse 23).

(C) The Law of the Spirit of Life in Christ Jesus . . . . (verse 2, ch. viii).

Of these five, three must be treated as having an objective existence (*i. e.*, as working, independently of human action upon them), and the remaining two as having a subjective existence (*i. e.*, as consisting in the consent and adhesion of the human mind). The former three are Primary Rules and Ordinances; while the latter two are Secondary Motions and Assents of the thoughts and the soul.

The three Primary Laws are the 1st, the 3d, and the 5th of the foregoing catalogue: let us consider them in order.

A. *The Law of God:* the Moral Law: that one of all His Rules of Action, which He has imposed on Man as a moral being and a free agent: that Law in which there can be no change while Man remains what he is, and which applies to him equally in whatsoever state he may be, whether unfallen, in sin, or in the state of grace: this rule is an unalterable one, and has no respect to the particular relation which Man may hold thereto: it is made *for* him, not *by* him, and in itself it cannot be modified or affected by his action under it, although his relations to it may undergo wide change.

B. *The Law of Sin.* This is the rule and tendency of that root of Sinfulness which exists within all the descendants of Adam: the present disease together with its effects. This also exists in the flesh and the members, naturally, and without reference to individual action.

Through this law, infants die: through this law they are the fit subjects of the Baptism for the remission of Sin.

C. *The Law of the Spirit of Life in Christ Jesus.* This is the new and divine principle which is infused into the nature, and kept alive through the Holy Sacraments as instruments: this principle considered as involving its cognate powers and privileges, as, *e. g.*, the strength to keep the Law of God; the blessing of filiation and adoption, and the assurance of being dealt with as children, and not as bond-slaves; the effectual result of transformation into the likeness of the Lord Jesus. This, also, is independent of human action; for the baptized infant is under this new law from the moment of its regeneration in that Sacrament, and the introduction of this principle is into the *Nature;* while its effect upon the *Character* is a later and a subsequent result.

Such are the three grand objective Laws spoken of in this Section. We have now only to consider the remaining two, which are subjective in their character, and, in fact, express the consideration of the human mind upon the others, and its motions with reference to them. They are:

a. The Law of the Mind. By this is meant the proper inclination of the Better Self; the direction which the spirit of man instinctively takes, and would keep, if not under an alien and invading restraint. This is represented by the Apostle as being toward the Law of God. Between them there is the first relation.

b. "*Another Law in the Members.*" The Apostle gives to this no name: he describes it as warring against the Law of the Mind. It is not precisely the Law of Sin and Death; but (see verse 23), it is that "other law" which brings into captivity to the Law of Sin and Death. Manifestly then it must be the operation of the Mind and Will toward that Law of Sin; the appetite for what may not be had: and as the Law of the Mind is the assent of the better nature to the Law of God; so this law is the assent of the disordered and disorganized being toward the Law of Sin. Between these, therefore, the second relationship exists.

Finally, it is in the Law of the Spirit of Life that the remedy lies, for these unhappy complications and disorders. It strengthens the good and it weakens the evil. It prepares for the full triumph of the Law of the Mind, and makes inevitable the final destruction of that "other law," nameless, and fatal in its results, whereby we are given over unto death, and from which we cannot be delivered but by the Grace of God.

24. O wretched man that I am! who shall deliver me from the body of this death?

This is the culmination of the train of thought. The soul which thus cries out, is certainly not the regenerate and justified soul. But it is the soul fully awakened to its true state, ready for God's Grace, and desirous to receive it. Not simply the soul of the Sinner, but that of the aroused, penitent, converted Sinner, as it exists before (and only just before) it is visited by the blessing of Redemption in Christ Jesus.

"The body . . . . :" for the Law of Sin and Death is in the members. A reference has been traced, in these words, to that terrible punishment of ancient and barbarous times, whereby a convict was chained fast to a dead body, and left in that horrible situation to die, while the corpse turned gradually to corruption. Mention is made of this by Virgil (Æneid viii. 485–8):

> "Mortua quin etiam jungebat corpora vivis,
> Componens manibusque manus atque oribus ora,
> (Tormenti genus!) et sanie taboque fluentes
> Complexu in misero longa sic morte necabat."

25. I thank God through Jesus Christ our Lord. So then with the mind I myself serve the law of God; but with the flesh the law of sin.

The transition is here noted, in the words, "I thank God through Jesus Christ our Lord." It is a passage from death unto life: and the deliverance comes solely through the Eternal Son of God, Atoning, Risen, Glorified. But this is subsequently explained at length.

"So then:" in the new condition described, the person is now brought into full harmony with the Law of God; while yet, in the lower nature, and in the members, there still remains the influence of the original fault and corruption of the nature. For that fault doth still remain, even in the regenerate. And yet (viii. 1) there is no condemnation for it; since, in Baptism, the guilt of Original Sin is remitted for-ever.

1. *There is* therefore now no condemnation to them which are in Christ Jesus, who walk not after the flesh, but after the Spirit.

"In Christ Jesus:" to wit, by being baptized into Him (see chap. vi. *passim*).

"Who walk not, &c.:" two things are here mentioned as necessary to the complete deliverance of the afflicted person; 1st, his being outwardly received into the covenant of grace; and, 2dly, his full, subsequent compliance with its spirit and its conditions.

"Who walk after the Spirit:" who take for the rule of life the Will of God, which the spirit of Man learns of the Holy Spirit of God.

It is manifest, that there should be no break between chapters vii. and viii. The sense is continuous: the division between them should be entirely disregarded.

2. For the law of the spirit of life in Christ Jesus hath made me free from the law of sin and death.

The divine and spiritual principle which makes him who is baptized into Jesus Christ to be alive unto God. This is opposed to the Law of Sin and Death. Both have already been explained. The Spirit of God gives a new life to the people of God, and with it a new law and rule of living.

3. For what the law could not do, in that it was weak through the flesh, God sending his own Son in the likeness of sinful flesh, and for sin, condemned sin in the flesh:

"What the Law could not do." "Three things the Law can do. It can develope the nature of sin; it can become the occasion of rousing up natural sinful passions against its holy and divine requisitions; and it can condemn the sinner to merited punishment. But in the great work which is absolutely essential to his well-being, the work of his salvation, it can do nothing. It has no forgiveness to offer, no state of justification and acceptance to promise, no divine aid without which sanctification is unattainable, to give." (Turner.)

"Through the flesh . . . .:" Through the sinfulness and impotency of human nature which was subject to the Law of Sin and Death.

"In the likeness . . . .:" He does not say that Christ was sent in sinful flesh, but in the likeness: for He bare our infirmities, yet had no sin: He endured in His Flesh the penalties of sin, and suffered weakness, privation, anxieties, hunger, thirst, pain, &c. Thus He was "in the likeness" of that flesh of ours which is sinful; but His Flesh was in nowise sinful.

"And for Sin . . . .:" *i. e.*, to atone for it, to expiate, to take it away.

"Condemned Sin . . . . :" Overcame it, triumphed over, and conquered it; and thus overthrew and set aside its claim to hold dominion over men; brought it under the reproachful and condemned condition of a defeated and humbled adversary. All of which representations are clear and literal and just, because Sin is not an innate power in us, but a usurper which has intruded into the light and domain of God.

"In the flesh . . . . :" *i. e.*, in its proper seat, the carnal nature, the body, and the members.

4. That the righteousness of the law might be fulfilled in us, who walk not after the flesh, but after the Spirit.

"That . . . . :" in order that.

"The Righteousness of the Law . . .:" The holiness and spiritual obedience required by the eternal Law of God. The power to render this obedience is given in the Gospel. Yet this is not an absolutely perfect obedience, but such an obedience as is possible to a loving heart and an upright conscience and mind. God requires no impossible things of any creature; therefore, not a perfect and absolute moral obedience from any sinner, whether before or after grace received.

"Who walk, &c. . . . . :" A repetition of previous words. Marriott paraphrases thus: "So long as our rule and principle of life is not in our own carnal desires and inclinations, but in those spiritual truths which we are taught of God, and in His holy will."

"Fulfilled *in* us . . . . :" He does not say *by* us, but rather *in* us; for it is the Holy Ghost who worketh all acceptable righteousness in the soul.

5. For they that are after the flesh do mind the things of the flesh; but they that are after the Spirit the things of the Spirit.

He means to show that the power of holy obedience is certainly ours. To "mind" is, to be bent upon. As the ungodly and the carnal are bent on the gratification of their passions; so the true Christian is bent on obedience to the voice of God and the motions of the Holy Ghost.

"They that are after the flesh . . . . :" They who live according to the suggestions of the evil principle in Human Nature.

"The things of the flesh . . . . :" The interests, cares, and pleasures of this transitory life.

"They that are after the Spirit . . . . :" They who, being

brought under the power of the Holy Ghost, yield themselves to Him.

"The things of the Spirit . . . . :" The interests of the world to come: the promises of God; His Laws and ways; the Ordinances of His Church; the promises of His Word, &c.

6. For to be carnally minded *is* death; but to be spiritually minded *is* life and peace.
7. Because the carnal mind *is* enmity against God: for it is not subject to the law of God, neither indeed can be.

Simple statements of Christian experience, requiring no explanation.

"Is death . . . .:" *i. e.*, death toward God; for to him who lives for the flesh and the world alone, God is as though He were not

7. "Enmity against God . . . . :" Since man was made in the Image of God, his will should be bound to God's will, and his spirit should hold communion with the Spirit of God. But when the flesh rebels and acts separately, the spirit and mind take a position of hostility toward the Almighty.

8. So then they that are in the flesh cannot please God.
9. But ye are not in the flesh, but in the Spirit, if so be that the Spirit of God dwell in you. Now if any man have not the Spirit of Christ, he is none of his.

8. "In the flesh . . . . :" in the carnal state just described.

9. "Ye . . . . :" *i. e.*, who have by Baptism put on Christ.

"Are not, &c. . . . . :" Are freed from your natural fallen condition, and made alive in the Holy Ghost. Formally, all the baptized are in the Spirit: effectually, those only are, who, having been so made partakers of the heavenly gift, do walk according to their calling.

"Now if any man, &c. . . . . :" The Apostle intends this as a general remark; he is speaking of classes, of Christians as a mass, the gift of the Spirit of Christ is the common privilege and blessing of all Christ's people. This should not be taken as intended to limit the mercy of God, but rather to show its width of application to men. Paraphrase verses 8 and 9 thus:—"They who are in their natural condition cannot please God, by obeying Him and doing His will, for they have not the power. But ye are not in that natural condition, but under the dispensation of Grace, seeing that the Spirit of God dwelleth in you. For they who are Christ's must surely have Christ's Spirit. But ye are Christ's, for so many of you as were baptized into Christ, have put on Christ. Therefore being Christ's, you must have Christ's Spirit; for he that had not Christ's Spirit would be none of His."

10. And if Christ *be* in you, the body *is* dead because of sin; but the Spirit *is* life because of righteousness.

The Apostle still dwells upon the surpassing gift and the fulness of our salvation. "If Christ be in you:" this should not be taken as expressive of a doubt. "If" signifies "forasmuch as," or "since;" just as in Colossians, iii. 1; where the same word cannot be intended to have a hypothetical sense, but forms a mark of reference to the previous assertion that they were indeed risen with Christ. "Since, therefore, Christ is in you, and you in Christ, as baptized members of His Mystical Body the Church."

Observe, that the Apostle is enlarging upon and explaining God's plan of salvation; and not, in anywise, considering the application of that salvation to individual cases, nor regarding particular persons with reference to their improvement or neglect of their advantages.

"The body . . , .:" *i. e.*, the material part of man; the earthly house of this tabernacle; the literal and actual body.

"Is dead . . . .:" Remains mortal; must die; is liable to death, bears all natural infirmities, and will return to dust.

"Because of Sin . . . .:" by reason of, or, in consequence of, the Law of Sin and Death in the members.

"The Spirit . . . .:" the spiritual and immaterial part of our nature.

"Is life . . . . :" is in a living condition; is not like the body, but lives, and shall live on.

"Because of righteousness . . . .:" through the operation of the Law of the Spirit of life in Christ Jesus.

The whole thought seems to be: that, when we are made partakers of the blessing of God through the Gospel, the mortal part of us still remains liable to corruption and decay; but the decay and loss cannot pass beyond the place of their present influence, because the spiritual part is made fully alive unto God, and delivered from that death which ought to result, as a necessary consequence, from union with the corruptible and dying humanity. Christians must look for no exemption from the evils and trials incident to mortality.

11. But if the Spirit of him that raised up Jesus from the dead dwell in you, he that raised up Christ from the dead shall also quicken your mortal bodies by his Spirit that dwelleth in you.

An enlargement, and a very glorious one, of the thought in the preceding verse.

"If . . . . :" again understand it as meaning "since."

"Shall also quicken, &c. . . . . :" A promise that the gift of life and immortality through Christ shall not be limited to our souls, but shall also be at last, after a long time, extended even to the mortal bodies. The allusion must be to the "resurrection of the body," which is an article of the true Catholic faith.

Christ's resurrection implies that of all who are in Him. The same power, the same Spirit, the same God, who raised Him up, shall, at the last day, raise up also His faithful people.

12. Therefore, brethren, we are debtors, not to the flesh, to live after the flesh.

13. For if ye live after the flesh, ye shall die: but if ye through the Spirit do mortify the deeds of the body, ye shall live.

"Therefore . . . . :" in view of all that has been said.

"The Flesh . . . . :" the carnal nature in its condition of enmity against God.

"Debtors, &c. :" We have no further obligations toward that carnal nature, that we should obey it. No one may sin, under the pretence that he is following the Law of Nature in doing so. There are no laws of nature so pressing or exacting, as to require us to sin, that they may be gratified. All the positions of the Materialist, the Epicurean, the Sensualist, of this or any other period, are invaded and destroyed by this verse.

"Mortify the deeds, &c. :" This, in opposition to any and all human systems, is the rule of the Catholic Faith. As Christ suffered, so must we. As He brought the Flesh into subjection, so must we. The Cross of the Lord is the perpetual symbol of the disciple. Mortification, discipline, penance; these are the exercises concerning which we are debtors.

"Die . . . . live." Death is the result of Sensual Indulgence and of obedience to the laws of the material being. Life comes to us from mortification of the flesh, and godly and Christian discipline of our unruly members.

It might be thought, from the turn which these remarks

are taking, that we were about to be placed again under some such system as that, whereof the Apostle has proved, that it could never bring Salvation to man. The thought of bodily mortification, of discipline, &c., might suggest again the thought of bondage to a taskmaster. The Apostle next proceeds to correct this impression. He shows, that we are adopted to be the children of God; that the relations between Him and us, are not as those between master and slave, but as those between parent and child; and that, although we are required to obey the holy law and to mortify the evil flesh, yet that our service must be the service of children, free from fear of God as a tyrannical ruler, and full of love and affectionate zeal.

14. For as many as are led by the Spirit of God, they are the sons of God.

Render, as in chapter vi., verse 3. The Law of the Spirit of Life in Christ Jesus, whereby one is free from the Law of Sin and of Death, is a law of Adoption and Sonship. All the baptized are regarded as members of Christ, children of God, and inheritors of the Kingdom of Heaven, and will be treated with tenderness and allowance as such: the law of the sons of God is a law of love.

15. For ye have not received the spirit of bondage again to fear; but ye have received the Spirit of adoption, whereby we cry, Abba, Father.

16. The Spirit itself beareth witness with our spirit, that we are the children of God:

We have not been brought into a second system of literal bondage, wherein dread and terror should be the prevailing sentiments. But we are adopted of God, and taught to call Him "Our Father." He will therefore deal with us as with sons.

We have a double proof of this happy condition; an outward evidence, and an inward. The Holy Ghost, impressing on us the glad tidings; and our own hearts and consciences acknowledging and rejoicing in the truth. The Holy Spirit, speaking through the Scriptures and the System of the Church, declares and affirms our acceptance and adoption of God. And the mind and spirit of the believer find internal evidence of the blessed spiritual change. "With," should be understood to mean "together with."

"A *feeling* of acceptance, amounting even to assurance, is happily not the test of filiation laid down in Scripture;

for such a test must ever be uncertain, and often dependent on physical condition and natural temperament."

17. And if children, then heirs; heirs of God, and joint-heirs with Christ; if so be that we suffer with *him*, that we may be also glorified together.

The full development of this thought of our adoption as the Lord's own children, is herein contained: ours is, so far as the nature of the case will admit, a complete identification with Christ; so as that He is the Elder Brother, the First-born, and we are after Him and very near Him, and, being here partakers of His sufferings, we shall also hereafter enter into His Glory. As He said, "The glory which Thou gavest Me, I have given unto them." Christ and His People are one.

18. For I reckon that the sufferings of this present time *are* not worthy *to be compared* with the glory which shall be revealed in us.

The thought suggested in the latter half of the preceding verse is here carried out.

"I reckon . . . .:" I consider; I feel assured.

"In us . . . .:" Perhaps, and probably, a reference to the redemption of the mortal body.

As Christ was transfigured; as He ascended bodily to Heaven, and as He shall come again in His Glorified Body; so may the bodies of His Saints be the instruments of manifesting a corresponding glory. "For there is a natural body, and there is a spiritual body."

"Shall be revealed . . . .:" Hereafter, in the day of Christ's final exaltation and triumph. But yet this glorifying is already commenced. For see S. John xvii. 22, and Rom. viii. 30; also 2 Peter i. 4. This glorifying must, of course, take an outward and visible form, where it may be seen of all; and likewise it must have an inward effect for blessedness and joy of soul and spirit, since it is here spoken of as the ultimate offset to all the sufferings of this world.

The end of this section now approaches. The Apostle seems to dwell especially on the fact which he has stated, of the adoption of mortal men to be the sons of God; of the passing away of all the former relations of fear and terror, and of the triumph of Divine Love as the great mediating principle between the demands of the Eternal Holiness of the Law, and the shortcomings and offences of the sinner. He glances at the mournful past; then recurs to the merciful visitation of the Lord; and finally celebrates the Divine Love in a triumphal anthem of praise.

19. For the earnest expectation of the creature waiteth for the manifestation of the sons of God.

"The manifestation of the sons of God . . . . :" The showing, or declaring the happy and blessed condition of mortals, as recovered by the mercy of God, and made His own children. This manifestation is already made, in its beginnings; and it may be contemplated by faith and dwelt on in hope; but it cannot be complete until the Resurrection shall have occurred; and when it shall have been beheld at length, all these initiations and first steps toward it may haply show as nothing. Neither can its manner be comprehended: for "it doth not yet appear what we shall be."

"The creature . . . . :" This must mean, primarily, and mainly, the Human Race: and secondarily we may include other works of God so far as they were capable of being affected by human transgression.

"Waiteth, &c. . . . :" Earnestly desires and looks forward to. The Human Race is represented as striving for some unknown good, which could not be realized until God's salvation, with its results, was clearly disclosed. We must not suppose them to have looked precisely for what has come. Theirs was a groping after somewhat better; they were wretched, and they needed relief; but how the aid should come, or what its nature should be, they could not have known.

"The creature . . . :" The Human Race.

20. For the creature was made subject to vanity, not willingly, but by reason of him who hath subjected *the same* in hope,

"Was made subject to vanity . . . :" Vanity means emptiness. For a creature to be made subject to vanity, is, for it to fall from all hope of a high and worthy destiny, and to have its career and the order of its natural development suddenly cut short and reduced to blankness and vacuity. See Job xvii. 11; "My days are past, my purposes are broken off, even the thoughts of my heart:" and further, 15, "Where is now my hope? as for my hope, who shall see it?" Reduction to complete emptiness, uselessness, and unprofitableness, is the thought.

"Not willingly . . . . :" Because, although the act was wilful, yet its consequences were not fully perceived: if they could have been, the impulse would have been to have recoiled from the act with horror. Self-destruction involves a contradiction, and seems to be an impossibility, if the mind be sane. No man would willingly ruin himself. The fall into this state of vanity was not from the calm, dispassionate choice, and original prompting or *proprio motu* of the victim.

"By reason of him who hath subjected the same." But it was through the act of another party, to wit, through the temptations and secret arts of the Adversary of Mankind, the Devil and Satan, the Enemy of all good.

"In hope . . . . :" These words do not depend on the word "subjected:" they should be taken as standing by themselves, and as expressing, in the logical order, a complete and distinct idea in addition: the Human Race, fallen through the seductions of the enemy, were not left to utter despair; but hope still remained to them, through the promise made in the very hour of the fall. Their condition, however deplorable and unhappy, was not, however, barren of all hope and expectation of a future deliverance.

21. Because the creature itself also shall be delivered from the bondage of corruption into the glorious liberty of the children of GOD.

Because they had a sure, though not fully defined, knowledge of such a redemption from the bondage, in which they where held. "The bondage of corruption;" the bondage to a power tending to reduce them to corruption, ruin, and decay.

"The bondage of corruption . . . :" The Law of Sin and Death in the members.

"The liberty of the children of GOD . . . . :" The state of those who in this world are under the Law of the Spirit of Life in Christ Jesus, and who, living thereafter, shall be glorified together with the Lord in the world to come.

22. For we know that the whole creation groaneth and travaileth in pain together until now.

A wider and fuller thought is now expressed. In the phrase "the creature," indirect reference is discerned to beings other than Mankind, as lying under the same sense of want of unknown good, and as labouring thereafter with an earnest expectation. Now it is affirmed that the whole creation sympathizes with the Human Race, and is in pain and distress together with them. We infer, from the language, that Nature has been affected by the offence of the First Adam. See how broad is growing the basis of the coming anthem of praise! See how deep a foundation the Apostle is constructing for his proposed monument to the

Glory of GOD! If the whole creation loses in Adam, then must it also gain in Christ: as the old hymn says:—

> "Terra, Pontus, Astra, Mundus,
> Quo lavantur flumine,"

speaking of the Blood of the Cross.

"Until now . . . . :" *i. e.*, until the time when the Son of GOD was manifested in the flesh; the beginning of the Gospel days.

23. And not only *they*, but ourselves also, which have the first-fruits of the Spirit, even we ourselves groan within ourselves, waiting for the adoption, *to wit*, the redemption of our body.

The last words, "until now," might suggest the thought, that the travail and the sorrow have already ceased, and that the deliverance has been completely effected. The Apostle hastens to correct such an impression, if it should exist; and to show, that the deliverance is but commenced, and that a great event in the future is to complete it.

"And not only . . . . :" understand, as before, the whole creation up to the time at which he was writing.

"Ourselves . . . . :" Christians, and members of the Covenant of Grace.

"First-fruits . . . :" The gifts of the Holy Ghost, such as are needed unto salvation in this world, are the pledge and earnest and first instalment of the full gift and endowment of the same Spirit hereafter.

"Groan . . . :" A milder expression than that in verse 22. Partial deliverance is denoted by this change in the language.

24. For we are saved by hope: but hope that is seen is not hope: for what a man seeth, why doth he yet hope for?

25. But if we hope for that we see not, *then* do we with patience wait for *it*.

26. Likewise the Spirit also helpeth our infirmities: for we know not what we should pray for as we ought: but the Spirit

Our state of salvation is not a completed one; but one in which hope remains to be exercised.

Hope implies that the object thereof is not yet in our possession. "Hope enjoyed is not properly hoped."

We must hope; we must live in hope of a better world, and await with patience the promised glorious change.

"Likewise . . . . :" To aid our faith and patience we have help from above.

"The Spirit maketh intercession . . . . :" "Qui facit per alium, facit per

itself maketh intercession for us with groanings which cannot be uttered.

se." The Spirit moves us to make our requests known unto God: and our petitions, intercessions, and groanings (see verse 23), being made through Him, are as though they were His.

"Groanings which cannot be uttered . . . :" Passionately expressed desires for that future blessedness which cannot be expressed in words. The human understanding is as little able to comprehend as yet the manner of the things to come, as the human eye would be to endure them, if suddenly revealed.

27. And he that searcheth the hearts knoweth what *is* the mind of the Spirit, because he maketh intercession for the saints according to *the will of* God.

28. And we know that all things work together for good to them that love God, to them who are the called according to *his* purpose.

"He that searcheth the hearts . . . :" *i. e.*, God.

"Knoweth, &c." Knows what the heart pleads for, under the influence of the Holy Ghost, and therefore deals with us not according to the imperfection of our prayers, but gives us more than we can ask or think.

We have now reached the beginning of a passage which fitly sums up all that has gone before, and prepares for that triumphal hymn of praise of the Divine Love, with which the section ends.

In effect, verses 28, 29, and 30, might be taken as a point of departure for an exposition of the entire Epistle, for what is said elsewhere bears on and refers to them.

What is the "purpose" here spoken of? The full and only adequate answer is given in Ephesians i. 9, 10. It is a summing up and gathering together all things into one Body or Communion in Christ Jesus; and Angels and Men are comprehended alike in the design. This is a Divine Mystery far surpassing our powers of thought, and respecting which the Apostles have given no explanation. But see Ephes. i. 4, 5, 18, 19; ii. 6, 7; iii. 4, 5, 6, 10, 15, 20; Col. i. 23, 26, 27.

Now the Apostle elsewhere says that this "purpose" was held in the Divine Mind, eternal ages ago. And here he says, that all things have been working together from the beginning, and shall continue so to work for good, towards its complete and entire accomplishment.

Who are "the Called?" He must mean, Gentiles and Jews alike and together.

For what has been the whole drift of the Epistle? Let us review it.

1st. the Apostle showed, that the whole world was in a state of condemnation. The Gentiles, who had the light of nature, did not render acceptable obedience toward God: and the Jews, although they enjoyed a clearer revelation, were not accepted of Him, because they did not obey their Law.

And yet, the Lord designed their Salvation, and had for that purpose, made known to all mankind, the Gospel system.

Under this system they were all saved, or to be saved, by Grace, and for the merits and through the work of Christ and of the Holy Spirit.

For Christ had given Himself a sacrifice upon the Cross for all mankind. And a fountain-head of new spiritual life had been opened in the Church. And men had been made the children of God, and filled with the power of the Holy Ghost, that they might serve and obey the Almighty, and so fulfil the end of their being.

All this great work of Restoration and Recovery had been expected and waited for by a weary and sorrowful Creation. And now it had commenced, and the power of the Spirit was engaged to its full accomplishment. And that accomplishment is sure.

For (to return to verse 28) this whole order of events has been lying for ages in the secret purposes and counsels of God. The Call of Mankind, their Recall to Himself, has been made, as it were, from of old: and all things work together for good to those who are embraced in that design. These, indeed, are *all:* but yet, the called retain the option of accepting or refusing the offered salvation.

29. For whom he did foreknow, he also did predestinate *to be* conformed to the image of his Son, that he might be the firstborn among many brethren.

"Whom He did foreknow," are the same as "the Called" in the preceding verse: all in general, Gentiles as well as Jews; all who hear, by His permission, the tidings of salvation as attainable in Christ. "Foreknow," means to love of old: to "know" is in Scripture language to love, to regard with tender affection. The expression is the same as that in 1 John iv. 9–11.

God loved our sinful race, and so "foreknew" us: and thereupon He did predestinate us unto the adoption of children in Christ Jesus. His predestinating decree is a general one and a conditional one: it is the expression of His will that salvation should be freely offered to all who will accept it, through the Incarnation of the Only Begotten Son of God.

30. Moreover whom he did predestinate, them he also called: and whom he called, them he also justified: and whom he justified, them he also glorified.

"Called . . . .:" To men so appointed to be saved, God vouchsafed the outward call of the Gospel, and the inward call of the heart.

"Justified . . . .:" And those who were thus called to that glorious state of salvation, were accepted of Him freely, and placed in correspondence with all the means of grace in the Church, in order that nothing should be wanting to them that their full redemption might be secured.

"Glorified . . . .:" And these, so called into the Covenant of Grace in Christ Jesus, were already endued with the first beginning of that glory which shall hereafter shine in transcendent excellency and splendour when the Lord Jesus shall be fully exalted in His Saints.

These verses have not the dry, low, limited meaning which the Calvinistic scheme requires in them. They do not refer to particular and absolute decrees: they do not express the idea of an elect few, fated, as it were, to be saved, and an equally elect mass doomed to damnation. The thought which they present is the worthy complement of all that has gone before, respecting the unity of our Race in wretchedness; the common Headship of Adam; the Redemption of all men in Christ; the offer of life to all; the abolishing of every distinction between Jew and Gentile; the Universal Benefit of the Gospel.

METHOD AND MEANS OF SALVATION.

Part 4th. Benediction and Praise of the Divine Love.

(CHAPTER VIII. 31–39.)

31. What shall we then say to these

This hymn or doxology, however beautiful, needs but little comment.

things? If God *be* for us, who *can be* against us?
32. He that spared not his own Son, but delivered him up for us all, how shall he not with him also freely give us all things?
33. Who shall lay any thing to the charge of God's elect? *It is* God that justifieth.
34. Who *is* he that condemneth?

It is the suitable and worthy conclusion of the whole train of thought.

"What shall we then say to these things?" To the things, viz.: which have been treated of thus far? to the whole wonderful plan of God, for good, toward them that love Him? to the tidings respecting the Incarnation, the Cross, the Resurrection, the Glorifying of the Lord Jesus Christ? To all these things, what shall we say? It would seem as though we had nothing left to say, but should rather be silent in gratitude and joy. For let it be remembered, that "these things" include the Manifestation of the Sons of God, a Mystery so great and glorious, as that it hath not entered into the heart of man to conceive of its manner.

"If God be for us, who can be against us?" That God is for us, has been hitherto abundantly manifested: nay it has been stated, that His Purpose of Good toward the Human Race was conceived eternal ages ago, and that He has caused all things to work together for good, toward the accomplishment of that end. It matters not, therefore, what powers may be arrayed against us: for God is with us, and He is greater than all.

32. "How shall He not, with Him, also, freely give us all things?" A natural and reasonable conclusion. The gift of God's Only Begotten Son, must certainly imply, or include, every other gift necessary to make His Mission complete in its results. And again, the gift of Christ is, as it were, the First-Fruits of the final gift: for in Christ, at length, shall all things be gathered into one, both which are in heaven and which are on earth.

"Freely . . . . :" as it were without money, and without price: for the gifts of God through the Gospel are not bought by man.

33. "Who shall lay any thing to the charge of God's elect?" The elect are all they who have been made, by Holy Baptism, members of the Mystical Body of Christ. These, the Ancient Enemy continually endeavors to circumvent and destroy. For Satan is the "Accuser of the Brethren:" and Satan also would have utterly destroyed

the righteous Job: he is the Adversary (as his name implies) of souls: and therefore it would seem that his arts are here referred to: but they shall not surely avail. Why not? Because "God justifieth:" God pardons and accepts the loving soul, whatever its imperfections may be; and Satan will in vain call attention to the errors and shortcomings of God's faithful people.

It is Christ that died, yea rather, that is risen again, who is even at the right hand of God, who also maketh intercession for us.

34. "Who is he that condemneth?" Sentence of condemnation, by whomsoever passed, shall weigh nothing against the decree of release obtained for us, through the Days-Man between us and the Almighty.

"Yea rather . . . . :" as though the Doctrine of the Cross were naught, apart from that of the Resurrection.

Here follow, likewise, the Articles of the Christian Faith as contained in the Apostle's Creed:

"He was crucified, dead, and buried;
"He descended into hell;
"The third day He rose from the dead;
"He ascended into Heaven,
"And sitteth on the Right Hand of the Father."

These articles constitute that Shield of Faith whereby we may quench all the fiery darts of the wicked one. His charges, his condemnation of us, are set aside in the fulfilment of the Divine Mysteries of our redemption.

35. Who shall separate us from the love of Christ? *shall* tribulation, or distress, or persecution, or famine, or nakedness, or peril, or sword?

All the work of redemption begins, continues, and ends in the Principle of Divine Love. For, see 1 John iv. 7–11. Nothing can separate us from that Love wherewith the Lord hath loved us, except it be our own lack of faithfulness. The Apostle enumerates divers forms of trial, and amongst them the *sword*, which proved at last the instrument of his own martyrdom, for he was beheaded. These "sufferings of the present time" are not to be compared with the future glory, and they can in nowise divide us from our Saviour and our God.

36. As it is written, For thy sake we are killed all the day long; we are accounted as

The thought might cross some mind: are not these distresses marks of the Divine displeasure? can the people who are so visited and oppressed, be

sheep for the slaughter.
37. Nay, in all these things we are more than conquerors through him that loved us.

really considered as enjoying the favour of God? To which the Apostle replies, that these and the like distresses are "no strange thing;" that they are upon us, "as it is written;" that the description of those who are known and loved of God, is that of people visited and sore distressed, yea, accounted as sheep for the slaughter: even as the Lord Himself was despised, oppressed, rejected, and afflicted. In all these things, how terrible soever they may be, we are made victors of evil, and even more than conquerors, through the power of the Redeemer; as He said, "in the world ye shall have tribulation: but be of good cheer, I have overcome the world."

38. For I am persuaded, that neither death, nor life, nor angels, nor principalities, nor powers, nor things present, nor things to come,
39. Nor height, nor depth, nor any other creature, shall be able to separate us from the love of God, which is in Christ Jesus our Lord.

A conclusion of great sublimity.

All things are enumerated in heaven, in earth, and under the earth: but there is no power among them anywhere, as against the power and prevailing force of the Love of God in Christ.

"Death . . . . :" the primal doom, the constant dread and fear of men.

"Life . . . . :" which may harm by "cares," if evil, or by "riches and pleasures," if fortunate: (see S. Luke viii. 14).

"Angels . . . . principalities . . . . powers . . . . :" names of the orders of the heavenly hosts, as in Col. i. 16. How could the Holy Angels come between us and God? It is but a strong figure, like that in Gal. i. 8. The possibility of such a thing is not intended in either place. This is all brilliant and glowing poetry; an anthem; a song of praise. Let us not hear the dull criticisms of a prosaic mind in connection with words so beautiful and so impassioned!

"Things present . . . . :" the whole order of this mortal life, up to the hour of death.

"Things to come . . . . :" the time between death and the resurrection, when the soul is in its disembodied condition. And then the eternity afterward.

"Height . . . . :" the Powers above us.

"Depth . . . . :" the Powers infernal; whatsoever and wheresoever they be; the Abyss, with its portentous shapes.

"Any other creature . . . . :" any created thing not mentioned before. Against one and all, were there occasion, the Love of God in Christ would eternally prevail.

Let us conclude the Section by comparing with some of these agents enumerated, the Articles of the Creed.

Neither Death shall harm us	For He was crucified, dead, and buried:
Nor Life	For the third day He rose from the dead:
Nor Angels, nor Principalities, nor Powers..................	For He sitteth at the Right Hand of God:
Nor things present, nor things to come, nor height, nor depth, nor any other creature	For He ever liveth to make intercession for us.

Wherefore, All Glory be to God.

Section Fourth.

God, and the Church, in History.

(Chapters ix., x., xi.)

SECTION FOURTH.

It has been the opinion of some who have undertaken to comment on the Epistle to the Romans, that Chapters IX., X., and XI. have no apparent connection with the remainder of the work: they are regarded as a kind of parenthetical portion; incongruous; and introduced by the Apostle for reasons known to himself, perhaps, but certainly not obvious to any one else.

Such a view cannot, however, for a moment be tolerated. That any one with ideas so meagre, should have taken in hand to comment on this magnificent part of the Word of God, is unfortunate for the readers of his productions. For we are sure that the chapters in question have a close relation to the rest of the Epistle, and that they harmonize with the subjects discussed therein.

These chapters form a Section by themselves.

Their reference may be considered as a threefold one: 1st, they refer to the Apostle himself; 2dly, they bear upon the nation of Israel; and 3dly, they have a general application to all sorts and conditions of men.

Let us regard the position of the Apostle. He was, at that time, the most eminent of all the converts from Judaism to Christianity. He had been distinguished among his own people, for birth, talents, learning, and zeal: and his defection to the faith in Christ was for them a telling blow. Their rage against him ran to unusual lengths; so that he was represented, not merely as a renegade and an apostate, but also as retaining no interest whatever in his former connections, as abhorring his former co-religionists, and as being alienated, in respect to sympathy and charity, from Israel. From these unjust suspicions the Apostle might naturally desire to clear himself, as opportunity was afforded.

2dly. It must be remembered, that the calling of the Gentiles implied a rejection of Israel. The Jews felt this; and were hindered by it from embracing the Gospel. They perceived, as the necessary consequence of the Apostle's teaching, that Israel was no longer to be regarded as the Chosen People of God; that Jew and Gentile were to stand thenceforth upon the same footing before the Almighty on the score of acceptance with Him; that although Jews might be saved, yet they who were saved would probably be few compared to the bulk of the nation; that in their national character, therefore, the House of Israel had completed their history, and must yield the ground to a wider system. All which ideas were the last that the mind of a Jew could accept or entertain. For they regarded the Covenant between themselves and the Almighty to be on this wise: that God was held and bound to them by the very terms thereof, and that it was indissoluble while they fulfilled their part of its conditions; which fulfilment they never doubted that they had accomplished, since they made it to stand mainly in the rendering of acts of formal and ritual obedience, and not in the pure and spiritual worship and service of conscience, heart, and life. Therefore the Apostle must meet this difficulty, and show that God was not to be charged with injustice in doing to Israel as He had done; and he must also show that they had misunderstood the meaning of the acts of God, and that the whole course of His dealings with them, would, if accurately construed, have prepared them for the conclusions which had at length been reached.

And, 3dly. It is to be observed,—regarding the whole subject in the widest point of view,—that the History of Israel was but the history of all finite instrumentalities, by the use of which Almighty God works out His grand designs. In that history there is a lesson for the world at large. The Apostle has been writing, with reference to that Purpose of God which was conceived eternal ages ago, and which was, in the beginning of the Gospel Dispensation, more clearly made known to men. He has told us, that God has been making all things to work together, from the beginning, with a view to its progress and ultimate accomplishment. Now let us consider, that this Great Development has been slowly carried on through the use of human agents. It is, or seems to be, inevitable, that many of those agents should be crushed and overborne by the magnificence of the scheme in which they were unconsciously involved. No man could advance a claim to the mercy of God, since all were sinners alike. God might, without injustice, choose or reject, at will: He might, with absolute equity, select the instruments with which He would work, and those selected should have no better claim on Him than those refused. And in the prosecution of the designs of the Infinite, it seems the most natural of all things, that the Finite should break down and fail. Israel had been chosen to bear a part in the grand development to which the Apostle refers. There was no antecedent reason why Israel should be chosen, any more than Egypt, or Canaan, or Assyria: for merit does not live as from Man to God. Therefore, Israel had no right to glory in its election to that work which it actually performed. But Israel failed. That was not surprising: it belongs to the Finite to fail. The human is perishable; the material must yield; the work, when tried by fire, will burn. Therefore, the ultimate probability that the instrument would be laid aside as no longer useful, should prevent any complaint on that score. Israel was a tool in the hand of the Almighty for the work which it is His pleasure to carry on. The tool must wear out: and, when worn out, it must be thrown aside. All complaints, against God, either on the score of His first choice of Israel, or because of His final rejection of Israel, are idle and vain.

But yet, Human Nature is one and the same. It is impossible, and it would be unnatural, for man to regard without profound emotion this mournful history of the wearing out and ultimate loss of the finite instruments in their association with the work and power of the Eternal God. It is a subject for sadness; for sympathetic grief; it is a sight calculated to stir to their deepest recesses the passions and affections of men. And we are likewise led to look forward, if haply there be any compensation in the future. We admit that God, in His Greatness, may deal with us as the potter with the clay; and that the implement with which He has wrought His vast designs, He may fitly fling from His Hand when He will. And yet we wish, that, if possible, it might be otherwise: that what has served Him might be kept of Him; that what is ready to perish might yet be saved. And thus, the rejection of Israel appears to the thoughtful mind as a heavy and a moving sight: so grand a people and so distinguished in their times, so illustrious through the neighbourhood of God's Glory and His Covenants:—so deep, so complete a fall! It is not in Human Nature to look unmoved on such a sight; nor is it possible to restrain the question, whether there may not be a future for that people of whom it was sung, "Judah was His Sanctuary, and Israel His Dominion."

These considerations prepare the way for announcing in brief the topics embraced in the three chapters now under consideration.

1st. The Apostle vindicates himself, and that in language quite natural, however strong it may sound. He says, that he would, if that were possible, have given up his own hope of everlasting salvation, if only his people might be saved. He asserts, not once only, the assurance of his affection and love for that Israel to which he had once belonged.

2dly. He shows, that no idea could be more at variance with the whole history of GOD's dealings with His people than this: that He, the Almighty, is accustomed to bind Himself to individuals, or to lines of men, so as to be held to those persons thenceforth. He adduces instances, and striking ones, from the national history of the Jews, to show the perfect independence with which the Lord had been acting from the first: taking up one and setting down another as He saw fit; and His ways are vindicated throughout by such a reference. Hence, too, the Apostle would seem to imply, that if the Jews had not been quite blinded by their prejudices, and if they had not failed to catch one of the lessons which their history was meant to teach them, they might have anticipated the very thing which had occurred, viz.: the rejection of Israel and the calling of the Gentiles.

3dly. He goes on to show, that there was a compensation for the loss, in a gain that should be; that the rejection of Israel was the rejection of a nation,—but that the individuals might live again in the Body of the Holy Catholic Church: and he even holds out mysteriously the view of a final repair and recovery of Zion, in the fulness of the accomplishment of the eternal works of the Lord. In connection with this subject, the Apostle also points a moral of the last importance, for the warning and instruction of the Church; showing that GOD's modes of action are, like Himself, unchanging; and that the rejection of the ancient family of GOD renders possible the similar rejection of the new brotherhood and society; and that such a possibility may be realized, by unfaithfulness to the trust committed to it. The Church of Gospel days is warned by the fate of that communion to which formerly the Covenant was granted.

Such is the large and luminous character of these three chapters: and such are the lessons enforced and commended to the attention of his readers, in them.

Let us now proceed to the commentary upon the section under consideration.*

1. I say the truth in Christ, I lie not, my conscience also bearing me witness in the Holy Ghost,

The Apostle first vindicates himself from the charge of indifference to his race. Very strong expressions of affirmation, implying the extent to which he considered himself misunderstood.

"In Christ . . . . :" As Christ is my witness: or it may mean, "on the word of a Christian man."

"Conscience . . . . Holy Ghost . . . . :" Cf. viii. 16. The double appeal is made; his own conscience, and the voice of the Holy Spirit unite in satisfying him of his sincerity in what he is about to say.

2. That I have great heaviness and continual sorrow in my heart.

2. To wit, on account of the rejection of his people.

3. For I could wish that myself were accursed from Christ for my brethren, my kinsmen according to the flesh:

3. Here is a verse about which commentators have disquieted themselves idly, and respecting which they have exhausted their arts, as though there were some extreme difficulty in it. There is not. The Apostle means, that, if such a thing were allowable, he would sacrifice his eternal hopes to save his people: it is a high and generous impulse, the sudden outburst of intense affection. Moses had said the same thing in his days, in behalf of the people; but the Lord rebuked him on the spot, and told him that such substitutions were not allowable.

"According to the flesh . . . . :" For S. Paul was also a Hebrew, and prided himself upon it. See Acts xxvi. 4, 5; xxi. 39; 2 Cor. xi. 22, &c., &c., &c.

* "The 9th chapter of the Epistle . . . has puzzled so many men much abler than the present writer; and, what is far more to be deplored, has been the occasion of dejection and of despair to many . . . . It is not the design to notice the various senses which have been ascribed to the different verses in the chapter. Far from this, there will not be reviewed or reconsidered to any considerable extent, what the author has heretofore taken the trouble to peruse; of the much greater proportion of which he judges it better to be ignorant than to be informed."—BISHOP WHITE.

4. Who are Israelites; to whom *pertaineth* the adoption, and the glory, and the covenants, and the giving of the law, and the service *of God*, and the promises;

Reflecting mournfully upon the theme, he recounts the past and faded glories of his nation.

"Israelites . . . . :" Their most honourable appellation; just as the Spaniards call themselves "Castilians."

"Adoption . . . . :" viz.: out of all nations of the earth to be God's peculiar people.

"Glory . . . . :" the visible Shekinah, in the temple; and perhaps the Pillar of Fire and Glory in the Desert.

"Covenants . . . . :" with Abraham, with Isaac and Jacob; with Moses; with David: Gen. xv. 18; xxxv. 12.

"The Giving of the Law . . . . :" from Mount Sinai.

"The Service . . . . :" the Tabernacle and Temple Services, with their entire Ritual System.

"The Promises . . . . :" of the coming of Messiah and of the blessing of all nations of the world in them.

5. Whose *are* the fathers, and of whom, as concerning the flesh, Christ *came*, who is over all, God blessed for ever. Amen.

"The Fathers . . . . :" the old patriarchs, the royal line, the prophets, and all the venerable names of the past of Israel.

"Christ . . . . :" Finally, the last and highest distinction, that from them came the Messiah, the Christ that was to be.

"Who is over all, &c." In vain do they who deny the Divinity of our Lord, seek to extricate themselves from the meaning of this passage; and strange are the devices to avoid giving to Him the Glory which is forever His due: truly heretics are at their wits' end. But it is clear and unmistakable; Christ is God over all, and, as such, blessed forevermore. And let all the people say, Amen.

6. Not as though the word of God hath taken none effect. For

How runs the thought? The Apostle's vindication is at an end. He was led on to magnify the glories and the privileges of his nation. All that splendour of dignity and honour is gone. Shall not God, who chose them for His own, who elevated them so highly, be chargeable now with inconstancy in abandoning them? And shall it not be said of His work, that it has come to naught? Not so, says the Apostle, not so.

Two questions, in effect, are proposed by the Apostle. The first is (verse 6), "Has the word of God taken none effect?" The second is (verse 14), "May He be charged with injustice?"

Let us consider the precise bearing of each question in turn.

The promises of God were made of old to Israel as a nation. But that nation is now rejected. Has then that promise been broken? Has the word of God *not* been kept? In reply to this he shows, that unto the fulfilment of God's word toward them it is not necessary that every one of them should have been saved: that God on the contrary had shown that such was not the meaning of His promises. He had made a covenant with Abraham and his seed: and yet Ishmael had been rejected, and the promise kept with Isaac alone; but the word of God was not broken. Again, the covenant was renewed to Isaac and his seed; but yet, Jacob was preferred before his elder brother Esau; and still the word of God was not broken. The question afterward arises, whether it is right to make such arbitrary distinctions among men: and the Apostle answers it by and by.

they *are* not all Israel,
which are of Israel:
7. Neither, because
they are the seed of
Abraham, *are they* all
children: but, In Isaac
shall thy seed be called.

Paraphrase thus: The word of God shall not be regarded as being without effect: for, just as it is clear to every one's mind, that not all Israelites are Israelites indeed, faithful and true; so it ought to be as clear that God's promise to Abraham was not intended to apply to every individual descended from that patriarch; for the promise that in his seed should all the nations of the world be blessed, was fulfilled in the person of one only of his children, *i. e.*, Isaac.

8. That is, They
which are the children
of the flesh, these *are*
not the children of God:
but the children of the
promise are counted for
the seed.

Ishmael was the child of the flesh: Isaac was the child of the promise. God had said, "In thy *seed* shall be the blessing." What shall we understand by the expression "thy seed?" Abraham no doubt thought that God meant it of all his children; for he said, "O that Ishmael might live before Thee!" But no: God's will was otherwise. The children of Isaac were counted for that "seed" to which the promise should be handed on. Observe, that in this chapter, it does not appear that the salvation of individuals is in any way referred to. The matter under discussion is, not the eternal state of particular persons, but the dealings of God with men in general, and with His Church. Nothing can be inferred of the everlasting condition of Ishmael, Esau, Isaac, Jacob, or Pharaoh, from aught herein stated.

9. For this *is* the word of promise, At this time will I come, and Sarah shall have a son.

A reference to the historical record of the event to which he had just directed their attention. This verse seems to be parenthetical, and adds nothing to the sense. "Isaac, as you know, was born according to promise, and by miracle."

10. And not only *this;* but when Rebecca also had conceived by one, *even* by our father Isaac;

And this is not the only case in point: that of Esau and Jacob affords another remarkable illustration. The promise made in general to Abraham's posterity, is restricted to Isaac; and Isaac's wife having given birth to twins, a distinction is made even there, and the promise is a second time restricted to one of those two, and that the younger.

11. (For *the children* being not yet born, neither having done any good or evil, that the purpose of God according to election might stand, not of works, but of him that calleth;)

This discernment between the tenants of the same womb was not made on the ground of any moral or spiritual difference between the children: it was determined upon, and announced to their mother, before they were born. The design of God was to stand and be carried out, irrespectively of the works of men, and solely in accordance with His *election* (*choice*) and call of those whom He had determined to make the instruments of His designs.

12. It was said unto her, The elder shall serve the younger.

13. As it is written, Jacob have I loved, but Esau have I hated.

"Loved . . . . hated." The words evidently mean, "I have regarded with more favour, I have regarded with less favour." God hateth nothing that He hath made. He distinguished between Esau and Jacob, showing to the latter a favour and an indulgence which He denied to the former.

Thus the Apostle has answered the first question. He has shown the Jews that they could not rightly argue, because of the rejection of Israel, and the calling and acceptance of the Gentiles, that the word of God had come to no effect, and that His plans and designs had been frustrated:

any more than it could have been argued, when Ishmael was rejected, that God's promise to Abraham's seed had failed; or when Esau was rejected, that the covenant with Isaac had come to naught. Their own history ought to have prepared them for what might occur. The fact that He had rejected the nation of Israel from being His peculiar people was not one for which they ought to have been unprepared. But now the second question arises: Can God be charged with injustice, for His rejection of Ishmael and Esau from being children of the promise in old times, or for the rejection of the nation of Israel at a later day?

The Apostle answers at once in the negative, and the object of what is said in the following verses, 14–18, seems to be to prove the point that God is not unjust. But how they prove this, does not so immediately appear: the verses are difficult, however we may regard them.

Some would so explain them as to take away the difficulty by tacitly denying that they are intended as proof, and considering them simply as illustration. Thus a very learned writer of our own paraphrases the verses as follows:

"From what has been said, can God be charged with injustice? Certainly not. But He acts according to His own pleasure, as He says, I will show favour and benignity to whomsoever I will. His plans all originate from and are carried out in accordance with His own will, so that their direction and arrangement do not at all depend upon human inclination or effort, but solely on the divine wisdom and benevolence. And, to give an instance of a bad man being made subservient to the divine plans, it is said of Pharaoh, that God allowed him to continue in order to display His power through the monarch's obduracy, and thus to spread His glory in the world. It is plain, therefore, that God so disposes all things as to promote His own purposes, extending His benefits to some, and suffering others to continue obdurate." (Verses 14–18.)

Now, however correct such an analysis may be, as far as it goes, it hardly seems to give us the full thought. There is left no place for argument: the Apostle's words seem to be regarded as mere illustration or affirmation. In addition to the bare sense of the words, as thus clearly and excellently rendered, let us seek for a line of reasoning under the surface, by which it is proved herein that God is not unjust. In effect the Apostle has selected the cases of Israel and of Pharaoh, as two, in each of which the power of God is indeed signally illustrated, but in each of which there is as signally displayed the sinfulness and unworthiness of men. And thus, an argument is at once suggested. For, if the acts of God appear at first sight arbitrary, yet we must admit that the creatures with whom He thus dealt, deserved, in respect of their sinfulness, no consideration at all at His Hands.

The clue to the argumentative character of these verses may be stated to be as follows. When the Apostle cites the cases, first of Moses, and then of Pharaoh, he must be regarded as intending to draw attention to the entire case as presented in the Old Testament. The thought which he would ultimately express is to be gathered, not from the ten or dozen words which he quotes, but from the whole portion of the Scripture from which they are quoted. This was the Rabbinical mode of citation: the first word of a chapter might stand for the whole chapter; and if a Rabbi should say, "the word, (naming it), means," he would intend to say, "the passage beginning with, or containing that word, means," &c. We have an instance of this mode of citation by S. Paul, in Heb. xii. 27. "And this word, Yet once more, signifieth," &c. But certainly he means, "the passage in the prophecy wherein that expression, Yet once more, is found."

So, when, in this place, the holy Apostle adduces a remark to Moses, expressed in a very few words, although sufficiently apposite as illustrating a way of action customary with the Almighty, it is impossible to show in those few words, any *proof* that God is not unjust: nor can an argument be drawn from the very few words quoted as addressed to Pharaoh. There is, however, an argument, and a satisfactory and conclusive one. But it lies in the whole history of Moses and the Israelites, at the time and place referred to; and in the whole history of the King of Egypt. What this argument is, in each case, it remains, after these preliminary observations, to show.

14. What shall we
say then? *Is there* un-

Unrighteousness in God? Surely
not. Far be the thought from any
man's mind. It needs no disproof.

righteousness with God? God forbid.

But yet the Apostle goes on to develope the truth.

15. For he saith to Moses, I will have mercy on whom I will have mercy, and I will have compassion on whom I will have compassion.

15. That is to say, God acts after His own pleasure; He shows mercy to whomsoever He will. But, beside this statement, remark the reference to the circumstances related in Exodus xxxii., xxxiii., xxxiv. An argument lies in the narrative there recorded; the quotation is from xxxiii. 19. God had scarcely given the Israelites the Law from Mount Sinai, when they revolted and rebelled, and made a golden calf, and worshipped it. The Lord would then have destroyed them from before Him; and, at that time, Moses offered himself to be blotted out of the book of the living, if that could have saved them. The Lord then announced to them His intention to withdraw from them: "and the people heard the evil tidings," and mourned and bitterly complained of the change in their circumstances. Here then is an apposite illustration of the rejection of a great number of the nation; for all but two of those persons perished in the wilderness. How does the Apostle prove the point in question, of God's Perfect Justice? By showing to the Jews (whom he particularly addresses in these three chapters) that, although the people were rejected, yet they richly deserved to be. And God Almighty is abundantly justified in whatsoever He may do or have done toward men, by the fact that all are sinners and ungrateful alike, and that no one is entitled to claim His mercy: He may show mercy on whomsoever He will, since all are without merit or title to it in His sight.

16. So then *it is* not of him that willeth, nor of him that runneth, but of God that sheweth mercy.

Rejecting the fanciful explanations which have been given of some words in verse 16, let us take it as expressing this; that God's great plans and purposes are carried on irrespectively of human wishes or human efforts in the matter, but according to His own way, and yet always with a view to mercy.

17. For the scripture saith unto Pharaoh, Even for this same purpose have I raised thee up, that I might shew my power in thee, and

Another instance is here suggested; the history of Pharaoh. He was a grave offender; but God has reasons for permitting the wicked to flourish. But yet the event justified the course

that my name might be declared throughout all the earth.

which was taken: he was preserved long enough to be an example and a warning to transgressors, yet his sins were great enough to cut him off from any claim to indulgence, and no mode of dealing with him could have been too severe. It is from the entire history of this man, occupying the first fourteen chapters of the book of Exodus, that the Apostle draws his argument, and not from the mere twenty-nine words here quoted. Before we can state the force and bearing of the argument, however, it is necessary to explain the words of verse 17, and the next.

"The Scripture saith . . . .:" that is, Moses, commissioned by God, saith unto him in God's Name.

"Have I raised thee up . . . .:" Some render as though it meant, "I have created thee, I have brought thee into existence." This is not the meaning in the original, and it gives a view discordant with all natural and revealed representations of the Lord. It means, "I have preserved, have allowed thee to retain thy power so long." (*Heb.*, I have made thee to stand or continue: *Sept.*, thou hast been preserved.)

"That I might, &c." "I might have destroyed thee, long ago, in just judgment; but I have kept thee in the throne which thou hast dishonoured, in order that My Power and Justice might have at last their full vindication:" this is the thought in the original, Exod. ix. 13–17.

18. Therefore hath he mercy on whom he will *have mercy*, and whom he will he hardeneth.

"He hardeneth. . . . .:" He permits to remain hardened. In the story of Pharaoh three expressions are used: God hardened Pharaoh's heart; Pharaoh hardened his own heart: Pharaoh's heart was hardened. When God is said to harden the heart of the sinner, we are to consider the sinner as having already hardened his own heart against God, and as being permitted by God, under judicial visitation, to remain in that condition.

The argument is clear. God permits the sinner to go to his destruction if he will: but God is not unjust therein, for the wicked provoke Him by their crimes. So, although He dealt as He did with Pharaoh, yet did Pharaoh deserve no better fate. And it is implied, both here and in the case of the rejected children of Israel who perished in the desert, that the Lord who so dealt with them must ever be consistent with Himself, and may therefore be expected to discard and destroy any people, any race, or any individual, who may not fulfil what was required according to his or their call and election of God.

Thus, therefore, do we explain verses 14–18; as intended 1stly, to express, by examples taken from the Old Testament history, the thought, that the Almighty deals as He chooses with the children of men, irrespectively of any thing but His own good pleasure; and, 2dly, that He cannot be taxed with injustice in that thing, because their sins have cut them off from claim on Him, and have rendered them "vessels fitted for destruction."

A captious objector is introduced: we are reminded of chapter iii. 1–5. This objector sees and speaks to the surface-meaning of what has been said: if he likewise understood the deeper thought, that would have irritated him still more, although he makes no reference to it.

19. Thou wilt say then unto me, Why doth he yet find fault? For who hath resisted his will?

The objection is as follows: The Apostle has asserted that God plans as He will, and that His plans cannot be altered nor His purposes set aside by man. Why then should He find fault with, and condemn, and punish men, who are helpless before His irresistible will? Our conduct, although it be evil like that of Pharaoh or of unbelieving Israel, does yet subserve the purposes of the Almighty: why find fault with us then?

20. Nay but, O man, who art thou that repliest against God? Shall the thing formed say to him that formed *it*, Why hast thou made me thus?
21. Hath not the pot-

The reply of the Apostle to this objection is a twofold one. 1st, how absurd for man to set himself up against his Creator! The potter does what he will with the clay: although it is only in his hands. But we are much more in the power of God than the clay is in the power of the potter; for He created us; and He surely has a perfect right to do what He will with his own work. So, 1st, the objection

ter power over the clay, of the same lump to make one vessel unto honour, and another unto dishonour?

is idle and inconsistent. This illustration of the potter is of frequent occurrence in the Old Testament: see, *e. g.*, the 18th chapter of Jeremiah. The reference is clear: the vessel which comes not from the wheels as the maker would have it, is flung aside, and another is commenced: so was the House of Israel rejected because it had not proved faithful to that which was committed to its trust.

22. *What* if GOD, willing to shew *his* wrath, and to make his power known, endured with much long-suffering the vessels of wrath fitted to destruction:
23. And that he might make known the riches of his glory on the vessels of mercy, which he had afore prepared unto glory,
24. Even us, whom he hath called, not of the Jews only, but also of the Gentiles?

And 2dly, the Apostle replies, that the rejection of unbelieving Israel was not a ground of complaint; because the Lord had borne with them far longer than they deserved, and for this they ought to have been thankful. Paraphrase the sentence thus: What if GOD, although intending eventually to display His power and to exercise due judgment, in wrath, upon the ungodly, did yet with wonderful forbearance, long tolerate the sinners who provoked Him by their deeds, showing themselves ripe for judgment:—hath He not a perfect right to do this? And, again; hath He not an equally perfect right to grant to others the riches of His mercy and grace, even unto such, whosoever they be, as show themselves to be worthy of His good and precious gifts, and instruments fitted for the carrying on of His purposes of good?

"Vessels of wrath . . . . of mercy . . . :" Terms suggested by the comparison of the potter: vessels good and useful for their purposes; vessels useless and therefore fit only to be thrown away, or broken up and moulded over again: The "vessels of wrath" are the sinful and rejected Israelites.

"Fitted to destruction . . . :" It does not say how, or by whom; least of all does it say that they were fitted for destruction by GOD. It simply expresses the fact of condition. If we think again of the comparison of the potter; a vessel would turn out a failure, on the wheels, because of the badness of the clay, or the presence of some unsuitable and foreign ingredient: in the same way, the human instruments used by GOD fail and break down "by reason of the frailty of our nature," and by the presence within us of the alien element of Sinfulness: thus the parallel is complete.

"Vessels of mercy . . . :" The members of the Catholic Church, converts from Gentilism and Judaism alike.

"Afore prepared . . . . :" This does not mean "which God had fore-ordained unto glory." But it means, "for whose complete and perfect redemption and glorification, God has made all the preparations that need be or could be required." Just so, in Ephesians ii. 10, we read, in our translation: "Created in Christ Jesus unto good works, which God hath before ordained that we should walk in them." A round-about translation, and one which might mislead, where any Calvinistic bias existed in the mind: the words should have been translated: "in which that we should walk, God hath before, or previously, made all needful preparation." That is to say, He has appointed the Church to exist, with all the means of grace, in order that every needful arrangement might be made, and every facility afforded, for walking in holiness and righteousness before Him

25. As he saith also in Osee, I will call them my people, which were not my people; and her beloved, which was not beloved.

26. And it shall come to pass, *that* in the place where it was said unto them, Ye *are* not my people; there shall they be called the children of the living God.

27. Esaias also crieth concerning Israel, Though the number of the children of Israel be as the sand of the sea, a remnant shall be saved:

28. For he will finish the work, and cut *it* short in righteousness: because a short work will the Lord make upon the earth.

This part in the prophecy of Hosea manifestly relates to the calling of the Gentiles; and is introduced by the Apostle to show that the event in question had been foretold by their own prophets, and that they ought to have been prepared for it. And this from Isaiah, is as clearly intended of the rejection of Israel and the saving of but a remnant of the nation. And in this way he winds up all that has been said, by an appeal to the sacred books of the Jews, to which it would have been impossible for them to make any satisfactory reply, and of which they could not evade, in anywise, the force. These general remarks having been made, let us notice particular expressions.

25. "As he saith . . . :" *i. e.*, as God saith.

"In the place, &c. . . . :" to show,

29. And as Esaias said before, Except the Lord of Sabaoth had left us a seed, we had been as Sodoma, and been made like unto Gomorrha.

that God would thenceforth make no account of place; but as the Lord said to the Samaritan woman: "neither in this mountain nor yet in Jerusalem" exclusively, but everywhere, shall God have His faithful worshippers.

28. "He will finish, &c." He will no longer delay, but will hasten forward the work of judgment and of mercy, the rejecting of the unfaithful and the recovery and redemption of the promised remnant.

29. The preservation of the remnant of Israel is the leading thought, as before.

30. What shall we say then? That the Gentiles, which followed not after righteousness, have attained to righteousness, even the righteousness which is of faith.

The conclusion from what has been said in this chapter, from verse 24.

"Followed not after righteousness . . . .:" See the account and enumeration of their crimes and offences in chapter i. Yet, when the offer of the Gospel was made to them, they accepted it.

"Righteousness . . . .:" to God's gift, through the Gospel, whatsoever it be.

"Of faith . . . .:" to that gift, viz., which comes upon all that believe the Gospel.

31. But Israel, which followed after the law of righteousness, hath not attained to the law of righteousness.

"Which followed, &c . . . .:" Who strove, after a certain way, to fulfil the requirements of the system under which they were placed, have yet not attained to the objects had in view when they were placed under that system. Why not? well might the question be asked. The Apostle replies:

32. Wherefore? Because *they sought it* not by faith, but as it were by the works of the law. For they stumbled at that stumbling-stone;
33. As it is written, Behold I lay

Because they misunderstood the design of that system. The Law was their schoolmaster to bring them to Christ: to show them the worthlessness of man in respect of God; to convince mankind of Sin; to lead them to cast away all hope save in Him. But yet they had sought acceptance, under their dispensation, not as of faith and as of God's gracious indulgence, and through trust in His promises; but they had come to regard Him as their debtor and to demand salvation of Him as a right. And so they failed. And especially they stumbled at that

in Sion a stumbling-stone and rock of offence: and whosoever believeth on him shall not be ashamed.

stumbling-block of the lowliness and unworldliness of the Lord and of His Kingdom. Finally, the Apostle adds a quotation to show, from one of the prophets, that this their offence in Christ was foretold.

The 9th chapter of the Epistle shows to the reader, that God's promises are made, according to His good pleasure, and that it has not been His intention to bind Himself arbitrarily to any man or to any class of men irrespectively of that which is right in Him who is the Judge of all the earth: and the history of the Jewish Nation might have prepared them to expect their rejection in case of their disobedience, as well as the call of the Gentiles to take their place.

The 11th chapter treats of the question of the possible salvation of Israel, and leads us to consider, that although the mass of the people had been rejected on account of their sins, yet that in the remnant who had been converted to Christ, and in the children of God called out of all lands to be members of His Church, the true Israel of promise was to be seen, and the promises of the Lord were to be taken as fulfilled in them.

Between these two chapters stands the 10th; a short one, in part supplementary to the 9th, and in part preparatory to the 11th. In it the reasons are stated at length, why the Israelites had failed; and the calling of the Gentiles, as a fact foretold, is again adverted to.

1. Brethren, my heart's desire and prayer to God for Israel is, that they might be saved.

The Apostle reaffirms what he had stated before; his deep affection for his people and desire for their salvation through the grace and the means afforded by the Gospel of the Lord Jesus Christ.

2. For I bear them record that they have a zeal of God, but not according to knowledge.

A zeal; but misdirected. He states this as a circumstance to their credit. So, himself had once been zealous for Judaism and against Christ; but he says that he found mercy because he did it ignorantly, and in unbelief. Some allowance is to be made: to be lukewarm is worse than to be an open enemy. This zeal of theirs was a favourable sign, which the Apostle would turn to account if he could. "I bear them record:" I freely admit; I gladly concede that they are zealous: still they are wrong.

3. For they being ignorant of God's righteousness, and going about to establish their own righteousness, have not submitted themselves unto the righteousness of God.

"Ignorant of God's Righteousness." I prefer not to give to this term the stiff and quaint meaning, God's mode of justifying men under the Gospel. See the note on chapter iv. 13, for the full meaning of the term, "the Righteousness of God." They were ignorant of what God required: they thought that He wanted the outward formal service of their ritual system: they thought that to be circumcised, and to keep the precepts, and observe the days, and make the offerings; to give tithe of mint, anise, and cummin; to fast twice in the week and to give tithes of all that they possessed; was what God required. The scrupulous outward righteousness of the Pharisee was, in the eye of the Jewish people, perfection: nothing could be thought of better than that type of religion. See the remarks of the Lord on the Pharisees and Scribes, *passim*, for explanation of the term "their own righteousness." Do not let us be confused with vague terms of the School, while we can have the plain and practical comments of the Lord Himself. If any one desires to know what that righteousness of God is about which the Jews were ignorant; and what they considered to be righteousness; and how they sought to establish those ideas and opinions of their own; and after what sort they lived according to them; and what manner of men they became in consequence; and how far they were from attaining to the Righteousness of God: if one wishes to know these things, and so to have a clear and full commentary on this verse, let him leave all tractates and schemes on modes of Justification, which are for the most part unprofitable and vain, and let him read the 23d chapter of S. Matthew's Gospel; and these following places, to wit: S. Luke xi. 37–54; xvi. 13–15; xviii. 9–14; also the Sermon on the Mount, and especially v. 17–48.

4. For Christ *is* the end of the law for right-

"The Law . . . .:" Undoubtedly, the Jewish System is meant.

eousness to every one that believeth.

"The End, &c." Christ is the final object to which the Law referred: for it was given in order to prepare the hearts of men for the coming of the Great Redeemer. It was toward Him, that the whole system given by Moses was intended to point. He was the scope, the object, and the end thereof; and it had no meaning except as interpreted with reference to Him.

Christ is the End of the Law:—

1st. Because men were to be convinced thereby of Sin, and persuaded concerning the Righteousness of God, and led and sent to the Son of God, incarnate, as to the Fountain of Cleansing, the Author of Pardon, and the Head of their new and spiritual life.

2dly. Because all the ceremonies of the Mosaic Ritual symbolized Him.

3dly. Because in His Person He fulfilled the Moral Law in its perfection, and so gave to Mankind an example of the service in which God delights.

"For righteousness:" for pardon, for acceptance, for sanctification, for grace, for glory; for all that we need unto everlasting life.

"To every one that believeth:" to those, whosoever they be, whether Gentile or Jew, who will accept Him as their Saviour and Redeemer, and will fulfil the conditions required.

5. For Moses describeth the righteousness which is of the law, That the man which doeth those things shall live by them.

The Apostle contrasts the Law and the Gospel: the question is; in what would he make the difference between them to consist?

Some, and probably most, of the popular expounders, suppose, that he intends to represent them as at variance in respect to the terms; that he would say that Salvation under the Law, was an excessively difficult thing, while under the Gospel, it is, in the same proportion, easy.

To get this sense from the context, they take for granted, that, in the fifth verse, there is described an Absolutely Perfect Obedience. The language of the Law, they say, is this: Ye must obey, perfectly, absolutely, and to the least and last iota, if ye would live thereby. While the terms of the Gospel are simple and easy: only believe in the Lord Jesus Christ, and ye shall be saved. This is the quintessence of the Lutheran hypothesis. Faith in our Lord Jesus Christ is represented as standing opposed to Acts and Works of Righteousness: and it is asserted, as the reason why men were not and could not be justified under the Law, that it required an abstract perfection of obedience which no one ever was able to render; while no such requirement exists under the Gospel.

To which interpretation, we object as follows:—

1st. That this purely ideal kind of Justification, although conceivable by the imagination, is nowhere even hinted at in the Scriptures. To say that, in the passage now under consideration, S. Paul intends it, is to assume what one should rather try to prove. Again we repeat, that Almighty GOD has never required of fallen men an absolute and unswerving perfection, and that there was no such condition to Salvation under the Law. We rest this statement, 1st, upon the unreasonableness of the opposite view; 2dly, upon the absence of allusions to such an imaginary Obedience; and 3dly, upon the fact, that divers persons are commended, in the Old Testament, as having been perfect in their generations, of whom we know that all had the faults and failings common to humanity.

2dly. The language of S. Paul, by which he is supposed to be proving the extreme easiness of Salvation under the Gospel as compared with its great difficulty under the Law, is but a quotation, almost verbatim, from Moses. Whatever the Apostle says here about the Gospel, Moses had said already about the Law: and whatever the words prove of the Gospel as used by S. Paul, they prove equally of the Law, as used by Moses. Let us, therefore, examine them, where they first occur, (Deut. xxx. 11–14.) Where is the dreamy and unreal theory of an Absolute Perfection as required under the Law? For Moses said, of the Ancient Covenant: "This commandment which I command thee this day, it is not hidden from thee, neither is it far off. It is not in heaven, that thou shouldest say, Who shall go up for us to heaven, and bring it unto us, that we may hear it and do it? Neither is it beyond the sea, that thou shouldest say, Who shall go over the sea for us, and bring it unto us, that we may hear it and do it? But the word is very nigh unto thee, in thy mouth and in thy heart, that thou mayest do it." Now, whatever these words, as quoted, mean, the same must they mean as originally used:

for it is inconceivable that they express, in the two places, totally opposite ideas. Moses could not have intended to describe, in them, a system involving the utterly impossible condition of Absolute Perfection. For such a System, with its statutes, would have been very "far off" indeed; the mode of fulfilling it would have been "hidden," of a truth; nay, the very exhortation, "that thou mayest do it," would have sounded like irony, if not like bitter mockery. But Moses, in those words, described the Law: therefore the Law, as the Israelites understood it, could not have been that intolerable system which the imagination of later times has depicted as standing in contrast to the easy Gospel.

Hence we conclude, that the point of comparison here is NOT, as has been supposed, the extreme rigour of the terms of Salvation under an abstract ideal of Law, as contrasted with a surprising and confusing facility, under the Gospel of our Lord.

And yet, a contrast is certainly intended. In what does it really lie? We proceed to the answer which harmonizes with the convictions of men, and with the Catholic faith.

Two systems are here set side by side; and there are to be noted in them a Similarity and a Difference. Moses speaks for the one, and Paul for the other.

They are alike in this: that each was the ordinance of the same loving and merciful GOD; that each was made familiar to men; that each was near at hand, possible and easy of accomplishment, replete with good to those who would hear and obey. Each, in fact, might be described in the very same terms; and when S. Paul would set forth the true character of the Gospel, considered as a scheme of mercy toward men, he could find, for that purpose, no words more suitable than those in which Moses had previously spoken of the Law. Thus the two Systems resembled each other.

But in one most important respect they differed. Moses, in describing Salvation as attainable under the System which he represented, spoke of acts, deeds, and works alone. Whereas, Paul, in describing Salvation as attainable under that System whereof he was made an Apostle, speaks only of the Lord Jesus Christ.

The reason for this difference is apparent. Each spoke to what he knew. Moses, as far as he spoke, spoke well:

further than he knew, he could not go. He knew the duty of man to GOD, which never alters: and of that he spoke. He enjoined no impossible service. But yet, he knew not of any "full, perfect, and sufficient sacrifice, oblation, and satisfaction" for sin; and, being aware that "it is impossible that the blood of bulls and of goats should take away sin," and that "those sacrifices which they offered day by day continually could not make the comers thereunto perfect;" he was left in embarrassment, and his System was proved to be unsatisfying and incomplete. All that he could do, was to re-enforce the duty of obedience. But he could not tell them of a Redeemer; nor of a Cross; nor of an Atonement; nor of a gift of the Holy Ghost; nor of Sacraments effectual unto life. He knew only that men must do what they could, and obey GOD. But there he had to stop.

Saint Paul, however, knew more than Moses. He knew of the Lord Jesus Christ: and of His Vicarious Death: of the washing away of Sin in the Blood of the Lamb; of the Law of the Spirit of Life in Christ; of the Baptism for Regeneration; the laying on of hands; the Holy Communion of the Body and Blood of the Lord; of all the mysteries, gifts, graces, blessings of Catholic Christianity. Therefore, he could speak to far more than Moses. But yet, all these things resolve themselves, completely, into Christ: and to mention Christ, is, to imply all these; and therefore he needs but to speak of Him.

Christ is the Meritorious Cause of our Salvation. The Obedience of Faith is the Condition. The difference between Moses and Paul is this: Moses, knowing nothing of the Meritorious Cause, spoke only of the Condition. S. Paul, does not mention particularly the Condition, because he is lost in admiration of the Meritorious Cause.

We return to the course of the text.

6. But the righteous-
ness which is of faith
speaketh on this wise,
Say not in thine heart,
Who shall ascend into
heaven? (that is, to
bring Christ down *from
above:*)
7. Or, Who shall de-
scend into the deep?

No more need be said upon these verses: he who would understand their meaning, will gather it from the dissertation in the preceding pages, wherein the Contrast between the two Systems, in respect of Similarity and Difference, is fully set forth and explained. The quotation is from Deut. xxx. 11–14.

(that is, to bring up
Christ again from the
dead.)
8. But what saith it?
The word is nigh thee,
even in thy mouth, and
in thy heart: that is,
the word of faith, which
we preach;
9. That if thou shalt
confess with thy mouth
the Lord Jesus, and
shalt believe in thine
heart that God hath
raised him from the
dead, thou shalt be
saved.

9. Faith in the Resurrection is here mentioned as the sum of all Christian belief. And of course a statement such as this must be understood as implying all the acts and duties which properly grow from the root of faith. To believe in the Lord as raised from the dead, is to believe in the resurrection mystical whereby His people are risen with and in Him; and so to believe it as that one should thenceforth be minded so to walk as he hath the Lord for his example. The drift of it all is this: that the Lord is near at hand, and that His salvation is offered to all, freely, if they will accept it on the terms decreed and fore-arranged by the Almighty power and love.

10. For with the
heart man believeth
unto righteousness; and
with the mouth confes-
sion is made unto salva-
tion.
11. For the scripture
saith, Whosoever be-
lieveth on him shall not
be ashamed.
12. For there is no
difference between the
Jew and the Greek: for
the same Lord over all
is rich unto all that call
upon him.
13. For whosoever
shall call upon the name
of the Lord shall be
saved.
14. How then shall
they call on him in
whom they have not
believed? and how shall
they believe in him of
whom they have not
heard? and how shall
they hear without a
preacher?
15. And how shall
they preach, except

Belief in the heart; confession with the lips: these, the former sincere, the latter open and steadfast, shall avail unto salvation. And so the Scripture shall be fulfilled: and they who so confess and believe, shall never in anywise be put to confusion. "In Te Domine speravi: non confundar in æternum."

There is no respect of persons with God: Gentile and Jew, together and alike, capable of receiving the adoption of children. The Lord, who is the Creator and Ruler of all, is ready to bestow the riches of His mercy and goodness on all without distinction.

The interrogative form of the verses is probably to be accounted merely as a result of the Apostolic vigour and earnestness of expression. The thought is one: that God, who offers to men salvation through Christ, gives also to them every thing necessary for insuring the accomplishment of His design. Invert the sentence: God sends the

they be sent? as it is written, How beautiful are the feet of them that preach the gospel of peace, and bring glad tidings of good things!

preachers of the Gospel, whose feet are beautiful upon the mountains; they deliver the message of the Word of Life; the people hear; hearing they believe; believing they call on the Name of the Lord; so calling on His Name and looking to Him for salvation, they are saved through Him forever.

16. But they have not all obeyed the gospel. For Esaias saith, Lord, who hath believed our report?
17. So then faith *cometh* by hearing, and hearing by the word of God.
18. But I say, Have they not heard? Yes verily, their sound went into all the earth, and their words unto the ends of the world.
19. But I say, Did not Israel know? First Moses saith, I will provoke you to jealousy by *them that are* no people, *and* by a foolish nation I will anger you.
20. But Esaias is very bold, and saith, I was found of them that sought me not; I was made manifest unto them that asked not after me.
21. But to Israel he saith, All day long I have stretched forth my hands unto a disobedient and gainsaying people.

Perhaps, also, and probably, there lies here a latent reference to himself; as preaching to the Gentiles as well as to the Jews. For this it was in him, whereby his countrymen were especially offended: he preached salvation to the Gentiles: and so the Apostle intimates his divine mission: he must preach, he must go, wo is unto him if he preach not the Gospel of peace.

To discern a logical connection between these verses and the rest of the chapter, is neither very easy, nor necessary. They seem to be intended to show, by citations from the prophets, that the rejection of the Gospel by Israel had been predicted.

16. "They have not all . . . .:" *i. e.*, very few of them have.

18. "Their sound . . . .:" refers to the Apostles and their preaching.

19. "Did not Israel know . . . .:" to wit, that the Gentiles were to be called.

"No people . . . .:" Despised and thought to be unworthy of the name of a people.

"A foolish nation . . . .:" In the eyes of the Jews.

20. "Very bold . . . .:" Very clear and outspoken in declaring the truth.

(CHAPTER XI.)

A great mystery overhangs this chapter; a mystery which cannot be cleared up, as appears, until the end of the world shall be at hand. For the Apostle speaks of Israel in such a manner as to make it clear that he believed in their restoration, at some future time, to the Divine favour. When or how this shall be, is one of those mysterious things known only to Almighty God.

But there are other topics embraced in the chapter, from which we may draw instruction for our practical guidance; and especially there is a solemn warning to the Church, founded on the history and the fate of the Ancient People of God.

The principal matter of preliminary inquiry is this. The Apostle declares, that God hath not cast away His people. How are we to understand the term, "His people?" Shall we take it, as describing the Israelites as a whole? or shall we suppose, that it only refers to those of them who embraced Christianity?

Without attempting to review the arguments on either side, let it suffice to have observed, that, in the opinion of the writer, Israel as a nation must be intended, and not the small proportion of converted Jews. And that there is here intimated some grand and comprehensive design of Almighty God, whereby He intends to recover to Himself, at a time, and by means, not revealed, that ancient race which He "foreknew." To such a design, if it exist, would correspond the extraordinary fact, that Israel still remains, a separate people on the face of the earth; amalgamating with none, and preserving its individuality; although without a country, or a capital, or a national and political position among the tribes of the earth.

From this point of view the chapter shall be explained: and few could be found in the Sacred Scriptures more pathetic, more impressive, or more fitted to suggest the gravest thoughts.

1. I say then, Hath God cast away his people? God forbid. For I also am an Israelite, of the seed of Abraham, *of* the tribe of Benjamin.

The assertion of the Apostle is to this effect, that God hath not cast away His people.

But it is explained by some on this wise: that this should be understood of the fact that some of them had

2. God hath not cast away his people which he foreknew. Wot ye

been converted to the Gospel, and therefore that His promises were fulfilled to these. And so, they would give to the words such a sense as this: "God hath not rejected Israel: for, observe, I am an Israelite, and yet I am saved in the Christian Church; and so are many others; by which you may see that He has not cast us all away." But such a sense as this, is too weak to be endured: it makes of S. Paul a mere speaker of truisms: it lowers the thought to the veriest common-place.

We explain as follows: "His People," signifies, Israel as a nation, the Ancient People of God. When it is said that God hath not cast them away, it means, not utterly and finally, although they be for a time rejected. When the Apostle speaks of himself as an Israelite, he means: "I remember the glories of my race, and, as an Israelite, I look forward to our deliverance; I still am of Israel, to wit, of that Israel for which there yet remains a future."

2. "Whom He foreknew . . . :" Whom He loved and regarded with affection from of old. The sense is the same as that in viii. 29, to which refer.

not what the scripture saith of Elias? how he maketh intercession to God against Israel, saying,

3. Lord, they have killed thy prophets, and digged down thine altars; and I am left alone, and they seek my life.

See 1 Kings xix. 10, 14, 18. In a time of extreme depression, the prophet represented to the Lord what he regarded as the apostasy of the nation. But the Lord admonished him, 1st, of the existence of a remnant of faithful men in the midst of the great mass of the unbelieving nation; and 2dly, implied the continuance of the national life and existence with intimation of more favorable days to come. The application of this example by the Apostle would appear to be as follows: 1st, that there was even then a remnant of Israel, converted, and obedient unto the Gospel of the Lord Jesus Christ; and 2dly, that, for the sake of this remnant, and in respect of His own unalterable desire and will, God purposed an ultimate deliverance for the nation at large.

4. But what saith the answer of God unto him? I have reserved to myself seven thousand men, who have

5. "A remnant . . . . :" The Jews who had embraced God's promises in Christ, are likened to the seven thousand in Elijah's time.

"According to the election of

not bowed the knee to *the image of* Baal.

5. Even so then at this present time also there is a remnant according to the election of grace.

Grace . . . . :" The Gospel plan is evidently meant: the "Election of Grace," is the bringing men into communication with the means of grace offered in the Church. The "Elect" mentioned in Holy Scripture, are the members of the Church of God: the "Election of Grace" may be taken as a term expressive of those members of Christ collectively; and the term "of Grace" is intended to show the freedom and the peculiar merciful character of our redemption. The whole phrase may thus be rendered: "Even so, there is at present a remnant of Israel, saved under grace, as members of the Catholic Church."

6. And if by grace, then *is it* no more of works: otherwise grace is no more grace. But if *it be* of works, then is it no more grace: otherwise work is no more work.

An enlargement of the thought expressed in the very last word: "the election of Grace." As much as to say; if the remnant be indeed saved by grace, then is their salvation not the result of following the works of the Law of Moses; for if it were, the distinctive character of the Salvation of man would not be what it is. The latter half of the verse is a reversal of the terms: nothing is added to the thought: indeed it is doubtful whether that part of the verse be genuine.

7. What then? Israel hath not obtained that which he seeketh for; but the election hath obtained it, and the rest were blinded

"Israel . . . :" The nation at large.

"That which he seeketh for . . . :" to wit, acceptance and justification before God.

"The election . . . :" That portion of the nation which had embraced Christianity.

"Were blinded . . . :" Were suffered, judicially, to remain in the state of blindness which they had willingly accepted and which they appeared to prefer to any other.

8. (According as it is written, God hath given them the spirit of slumber, eyes that they should not see, and ears that they should not hear;) unto this day.

"According &c. . . . :" This condition had been foreseen, and referred to in prophecy.

"Unto this day . . . :" The connection may be either with the preceding verse, or with this: the sense is good in either way. When God is said to do thus, His judicial acts toward the wilfully sinful and perverse are denoted.

9. And David saith, Let their table be made a snare, and a trap, and a stumbling-block, and a recompense unto them:
10. Let their eyes be darkened, that they may not see, and bow down their back alway.
11. I say then, Have they stumbled that they should fall? GOD forbid: but *rather* through their fall salvation *is come* unto the Gentiles, for to provoke them to jealousy.

The quotations from the Old Testament are apparently intended to show, that GOD had forewarned them of the consequences of obstinate unbelief, and had denounced against them the threat of thus leaving them, by the imposition of a judicial visitation, in the state of darkness which they had chosen.

"Have they stumbled . . . . :" Have they been permitted thus to stumble at that stumbling-block of the Messiah (see verse 32, chapter ix.)

"That they should fall." That they should utterly, finally, and hopelessly perish.

"For to provoke them to jealousy . . . . :" *i. e.*, to arouse them to emulation. Such an emulation, if it could be excited, should not, therefore, be in vain. The "for" should not be taken as causal: as though the calling of the Gentiles were to the end that the Israelites might be incited to exertion: but it is another way of expressing this thought: "they have not utterly and irrecoverably fallen away, but rather the very call of the Gentiles might perchance arouse them to emulation and thus secure their salvation."

12. Now if the fall of them *be* the riches of the world, and the diminishing of them the riches of the Gentiles; how much more their fulness?

"The riches of the world . . . . :" The great gain of the world: the advantage of the world: the means of enriching all nations of the earth with the goodly heritage of GOD's offers of Salvation.

"The diminishing of them . . . . :" Not, the lessening of them numerically: but, the forlorn, wretched, and unhappy condition into which they are fallen. See Psalm cvii. 39, for the sense of the word "minished."

"Their fulness . . . . :" Their state of completed blessedness consequent upon conversion to the Gospel of Christ.

13. For I speak to you Gentiles, inasmuch

The remark in the preceding verse must be taken as potential. "The

as I am the apostle of the Gentiles, I magnify mine office:

14. If by any means I may provoke to emulation *them which are* my flesh, and might save some of them.

fall of Israel has been the means of benefiting and blessing the Gentile world: if this be so, how much greater blessings and benefits ought we to look for if their general conversion and recovery should take place!" Then the Apostle goes on to say, that he does not derogate from the importance of his work as the Apostle of the Gentiles, by such representations; nay, that he even elevates his work in importance; such great benefits lie on either hand: he magnifies the grace given to the Gentiles, because it shall be poured back upon Israel: and thus he not merely honours his work in the eyes of the Gentiles, but also strives, if he can, to make it productive of results toward his own people, if haply he might bring them to look upon the subject as they ought to do.

"My flesh . . . . :" The closest unity is expressed, and of course the deepest and most devoted attachment. So, when God would show us His love, and draw us to union with Him, the Word was made *Flesh.*

15. For if the casting away of them *be* the reconciling of the world, what *shall* the receiving *of them be*, but life from the dead?

16. For if the firstfruit *be* holy, the lump *is* also *holy*: and if the root *be* holy, so *are* the branches.

The Apostle implies, by the turn of the language, that he looks for such a receiving of them to God's mercy and peculiar favour again, as one of the mysteries of the yet unknown future.

"The first-fruit . . . . :" The elect remnant spoken of before.

"The lump . . . . :" The whole nation.

"The root . . . . :" The old patriarchs and fathers.

"The branches . . . . :" Their descendants, the Israel of the Apostle's time and day.

The thought of the Apostle seems to be, that Israel is still regarded as, in some sort, holiness unto the Lord; and that in a double way. 1st, Because of the old times when it was so of a truth, and for the sakes of the fathers: and, 2dly, because the "election of grace" has been accepted as a kind of offering of first-fruits, and so the whole of the nation is conditionally accepted therein; for the first-fruits, when consecrated to the Lord, imply a consecration virtual of all that, from which they are taken.

17. And if some of the branches be broken off, and thou, being a wild olive tree, wert graffed in among them, and with them partakest of the root and fatness of the olive tree;

18. Boast not against the branches. But if thou boast, thou bearest not the root, but the root thee.

The figure, or parable, is clear, although the Apostle may not have intended to express himself with precision in respect to the terms employed. The tree is the Ancient Church: some of the branches broken off, are the rejected of Israel. The grafts of the wild olive are the Gentile Churches. Surely the Root is Christ: for He is the Root and offspring of David.

18. "The branches . . . . :" viz., the branches which were broken off. "Thou bearest not . . . . :" Consider, or remember, that thou bearest not, &c.

19. Thou wilt say then, The branches were broken off, that I might be graffed in.

20. Well; because of unbelief they were broken off, and thou standest by faith. Be not high-minded, but fear:

20. "Well:" *i. e.*, supposing that to be the case: but the Apostle does not say that it is. And indeed the tone of the remark leads us to suspect it. For who shall say without presumption, that the natural branches must be broken off in order that the wild ones might be graffed in?

"Thou standest by faith." The figure is dropped: the realities are again before us. The Catholic Church stands only by faith: not in presumption or pride, lest there come a fall.

21. For if God spared not the natural branches, *take heed* lest he also spare not thee.

22. Behold therefore the goodness and severity of God: on them which fell, severity; but toward thee, goodness, if thou continue in *his* goodness: otherwise thou also shalt be cut off.

When did Apostle ever utter graver words of warning? And how sorrowfully, after years of schism, defeat, and loss, do they sound upon the ear! Whither shall we go for peace or rest, since the severity of God rests now upon the heads of His elect? What can we do, but cling to the promises of the Lord, believing that after some hidden and inscrutable way those words are even at this hour true, "the Gates of Hell shall not prevail against her;" and humbly making our petition, Benigne fac, Domine, in bona voluntate tua Sion: ut ædificentur muri Hierusalem!

23. And they also, if they abide not still in

"They also:" the nation of Israel at large; now outcasts, exiles, and wanderers through the earth, and yet distinct and peculiar among all people wheresoever they sojourn.

unbelief, shall be graffed in: for God is able to graff them in again.

"Shall be." More than a possibility seems to be intimated here.

24. For if thou wert cut out of the olive tree which is wild by nature, and wert graffed contrary to nature into a good olive tree: how much more shall these, which be the natural *branches*, be graffed into their own olive tree?

24. The probability and facility of their recovery and restoration are compared with the circumstances of their loss, in a hopeful and natural way.

23. "God is able, &c." The objection might be raised; how can the Jews be converted after so many years? how impossible a thing it would appear! The Apostle in reply appeals to the belief in God's omnipotence; as much as to say that this work requires no less a power than that of the Almighty.

25. For I would not, brethren, that ye should be ignorant of this mystery, lest ye should be wise in your own conceits; that blindness in part is happened to Israel, until the fulness of the Gentiles be come in.

"This mystery:" this part, this portion, in God's secret counsels and designs: the Apostle is speaking of somewhat into which the human reason cannot look very far.

"In part . . . .:" should not go with "blindness," but with "Israel:" the thought is, that upon a portion of Israel this night of gross darkness has descended, so that they should be shut out from the knowledge of the Messiah.

"Until the fulness, &c." Until the nations in general shall have been converted to Christ: and the implication is, that if this blindness is upon them until that time, it shall not remain after the time here specified. "And so," as the holy Apostle goes on to say, "all Israel shall be saved:" that is, Israel as a mass, as a people, in general; all of them who then exist, shall be converted to Christ, added to the Church, and placed in the state of Salvation. And then, the Apostle adds, shall be seen and understood the full meaning and the accomplishment of the prophecies of the Old Testament concerning the Redeemer of Israel and their salvation through Him.

26. And so all Israel shall be saved: as it is written, There shall come out of Sion the Deliverer, and shall turn away ungodliness from Jacob:

27. For this *is* my covenant unto them, when I shall take away their sins.

28. As concerning

the gospel, *they are* enemies for your sakes: but as touching the election, *they are* beloved for the fathers' sakes.
29. For the gifts and calling of God *are* without repentance.

For the present, Israel was left in enmity to God, for the sake of those who meanwhile might receive the blessing. But yet, for the sake of those who had gone before, and of God's early choice of them, they were still dear to Him. For His gifts and His calling, are things about which God does not change His mind. "Repentance," means change of mind or intention. So likewise in Heb. xii. 17, "he found no place of repentance," which means, he found no power whereby he could alter his father's mind or reverse what had been already done.

Almighty God neither changes His mind nor withdraws His promises. Men refuse, however, to be governed by Him; and through their own sins, they cast themselves away from the reach of His Compassion, and then it seems as though it were He that had changed when He visits the sinner, although it is not He but the sinner who is altered. So His love and affection were still toward Israel, and He would still have them to be saved.

30. For as ye in times past have not believed God, yet have now obtained mercy through their unbelief:
31. Even so have these also now not believed, that through your mercy they also may obtain mercy.

"As ye . . . .:" Gentiles.

"In times past . . . .:" before their call and conversion.

"Through their unbelief . . . .:" as a result or consequence of their refusal of God's mercy.

"Through your mercy . . . .:" through the mercy shown to the Gentiles: through the round of spiritual gifts and graces contained and offered in the System of the Catholic Church.

"They also may obtain mercy . . . .:" by being converted to the Faith in Christ.

32. For God hath concluded them all in unbelief, that he might have mercy upon all.

"Hath concluded them . . . .:" hath suffered them to be concluded, or shut up, in darkness and unbelief, for a time: in order that eventually He may bring them to light and salvation.

"All . . . .:" Classes, masses, are referred to: not every individual.

And now, the Apostle terminates all that hath been said respecting the Mysteries of Salvation through the Lord

Jesus Christ, with the glowing language of wonder, love, and praise. For the power of explanation fails; and the tongue hath no more that it can do, but to extol, and honour the Most High God, all whose works are truth and His ways judgment. "O Altitudo divitiarum Sapientiæ et Scientiæ Dei!" Well may he utter this earnest, thoughtful strain, and well may we, having learned, prolong it in the later ages of this world. In the Doxology with which the eighth chapter closed, there was celebrated the Divine and Eternal Love. Now, at the last, the Apostle rejoices in the Riches, the Knowledge, and the Wisdom of God, and his Soul doth magnify Him, whose ways, in this behalf, are of a truth past finding out. Three things are unsearchable: the wealth of the Grace of the Lord, so abundantly poured forth on all mankind; the Wisdom which hath ordered all events toward the everlasting welfare of the creation; the Knowledge which holds, as well the circle of all revelation thus far, as those more excellent things which lie yet behind the veil, and for which the praises of eternity shall not suffice unto enumeration. Into these three, the Reason cannot penetrate: none can comprehend them, whether Angel or Man. For who hath known the Mind of the Lord, in respect of that hidden Knowledge? Or who hath counselled with Him, in regard to the course of His Providential Wisdom? Or who hath given or rendered unto Him, save of that which He had first bestowed? So, then, let Men and Angels be still, that the Almighty alone may be exalted: for the Lord is in His Holy Temple, let all the earth keep silence before Him. For of Him, and through Him, and to Him are all things. Of Him, the Father; through Him, the Son; to Him, the Holy Ghost. "Origo, et Cursus, et Terminus, Rerum Omnium." The Creator, the Word, the Spirit; He in whose Image we were made; the God of the Spirits of all Flesh; the Beginning of our Strength, the End in whom we rest. Glory be to the Father, of whom are all things; and to the Son, through whom are all things; and to the Holy Ghost, to whom are all things. For they, the Eternal Three in One, are, to us, the mighty shadowings-forth of Omnipotence, Wisdom, and Love, whence all creatures drink in strength, intelligence, and blessedness. Therefore, with Angels and Archangels, and with all the Company of Heaven, and with that vast multitude, whom no man can number, of all people, kindreds, nations, and tongues, let us respond and, continually rejoicing, say :—

33. O the depth of the riches both of the wisdom and knowledge of GOD! how unsearchable *are* his judgments, and his ways past finding out!
34. For who hath known the mind of the Lord? or who hath been his counsellor?
35. Or who hath first given to him, and it shall be recompensed unto him again?
36. For of him, and through him, and to him, *are* all things: to whom *be* glory for ever. Amen.

PART SECOND.

THE PRACTICAL PORTION OF THE EPISTLE.

CHAPTERS XII. TO XVI. INCLUSIVE.

PART SECOND.

We have now before us that portion of the Epistle, in which S. Paul, having completed the grand review of the Manner of Redemption, proceeds to apply what he has said to the practical guidance of life in this world. However beautiful and instructive these latter chapters may be, they present but little that is difficult to understand: and therefore they shall be passed over with brief comment. He who should devoutly weigh and ponder them, however, and in whose heart the Holy Ghost should enkindle an ardent desire to lead the life which they describe, would surely not be far from the Kingdom of Heaven.

(CHAPTER XII.)

1. I beseech you therefore, brethren, by the mercies of God, that ye present your bodies a living sacrifice, holy, acceptable unto God, *which is* your reasonable service.

"Therefore:" As a consequence from all that has been said.

The Apostle has shown, that under the Gospel, men are received by God's Mercy; their sins are forgiven; the germ of a new life is implanted; all fears which might arise, owing to the lingering of the old disease in the members, are quieted; men are brought, through Christ, into union with God, and made partakers again of His Righteousness: THEREFORE let them yield themselves to Him who hath so called them.

"Your bodies:" In them was the law of sin and death; in them should be shown the triumph of Divine Grace.

"A living sacrifice." There is nothing unreal in true religion: it is an outward, visible, tangible, positive fact. The life must be God's. What less can express the gratitude we owe?

"Reasonable." This signifies spiritual. The offering of the body, is the true spiritual service. No system which rejects the forms of the Gospel can hope to keep the spirit of the Gospel. As body and soul are one man: so are the outward and the inward one living truth.

2. And be not con-
formed to this world:
but be ye transformed
by the renewing of your
mind, that ye may prove
what *is* that good, and
acceptable, and perfect,
will of GOD.

Let it not surprise any that this should be addressed to those who had already been taken out of the world and led to Christ. The divine order is not as that which our self-will invents. GOD's Gift precedes: and on the fact that it has been bestowed, is based the duty of improving it. The language of Modern Religionisms is this: Because ye live well, therefore ye are shown to be Christ's. But the old message was: Because ye have been made Christ's, therefore ye ought to live well. And thus, upon the FACT of their having received the heavenly gift in their Baptism, is based the whole system of love, prayer, and duty for the children of the Church.

"That ye may prove." That ye may be living testimonies to the power which worketh in you.

3. For I say, through
the grace given unto
me, to every man that
is among you, not to
think *of himself* more
highly than he ought to
think; but to think so-
berly, according as GOD
hath dealt to every
man the measure of
faith.

"Through the grace, &c.:" *i. e.*, he speaks, not of himself, but as he was moved by the Holy Ghost.

"According as GOD, &c." Recognizing the variety of GOD's blessed gifts; and how He makes allowance for us all, and deals to us as He will of the talents of His divine treasury. The measure proportioned to each one's faith; as it was said, "According to thy faith, so be it unto thee."

4. For as we have
many members in one
body, and all members
have not the same of-
fice:
5. So we, *being* many,
are one body in Christ,
and every one members
one of another.
6. Having then gifts
differing according to
the grace that is given

6. "Prophecy." This was one of the miraculous and extraordinary gifts of the first age of the Church. It was a gift which one might or might not use (see 1 Cor. xiv. 32): the Apostle would have it exercised according to a man's ability, not for his own advantage, but for the common benefit of all.

7. "Let us wait on." Let us conscientiously exercise it.

to us, whether prophecy, *let us prophesy* according to the proportion of faith;

7. Or ministry, *let us wait* on *our* ministering: or he that teacheth, on teaching;

8. Or he that exhorteth, on exhortation: he that giveth, *let him do it* with simplicity; he that ruleth, with diligence; he that sheweth mercy, with cheerfulness.

9. *Let* love be without dissimulation. Abhor that which is evil; cleave to that which is good.

10. *Be* kindly affectioned one to another with brotherly love; in honour preferring one another;

11. Not slothful in business; fervent in spirit; serving the Lord;

12. Rejoicing in hope; patient in tribulation; continuing instant in prayer;

13. Distributing to the necessity of saints; given to hospitality.

14. Bless them which persecute you: bless, and curse not.

15. Rejoice with them that do rejoice, and weep with them that weep.

16. *Be* of the same mind one toward another. Mind not high things, but condescend to men of low estate. Be not wise in your own conceits.

17. Recompense to

8. "Simplicity." Open hearted kindness; cheerfulness; liberality.

"Without dissimulation." No one should hypocritically feign what he does not feel: as the selfish and worldly-minded, who, for their own profit, or the gaining of influence, affect to care for others more than they do.

10. "Brotherly love," means "love of the brethren." While we must keep charity with all men, yet are our first duties to the Household of Faith.

11. "Business." This does not mean, worldly affairs alone: rather should it be understood of all, whatsoever a man findeth to do in this world, according to the will of God: in every thing should we be earnest.

12. "Hope." The glorious hope afforded in the Gospel.

16. Do not have mere selfish aims: but desire the common good, and contribute all that you can toward securing the greatest benefits for the largest number. He who lives unto himself, is unlike his Lord: and Selfishness is as a great gulf between the soul and Heaven.

"Condescend." This is not to be understood in our modern way, as though a kind of lowering one's self were implied; for that involves a good opinion of one's self, and a feeling of being above others. But it means, to go along with the humble, and to be content, if need so require, with their lot: for "why is earth and ashes proud?" and who is aught but insignificant to the Eye of the Almighty?

17. "Provide, &c.:" *i. e.*, take care that all, in your life and manners, be becoming your Christian calling

no man evil for evil. Provide things honest in the sight of all men.
18. If it be possible, as much as lieth in you, live peaceably with all men.
19. Dearly beloved, avenge not yourselves, but *rather* give place unto wrath: for it is written, Vengeance *is* mine; I will repay, saith the Lord.
20. Therefore if thine enemy hunger, feed him; if he thirst, give him drink: for in so doing thou shalt heap coals of fire on his head.
21. Be not overcome of evil, but overcome evil with good.

and profession, lest scandal come to the Church.

18. Well might the Apostle speak thus: for few ever knew better than he how hard it is to live peaceably and in charity with this troublesome and ungodly world.

19. "Give place unto wrath:" *i. e.*, do not let your headlong wrath go forward to its own vindication; but restrain it, hold it in; and leave the way free, and so give place, to the ultimate but sure visitation of the Wrath of Almighty God.

20. "Thou shalt heap, &c." Compare Proverbs xxv. 21, 22. The same thought is expressed: it is better for us to leave things to God, than to take them into our own hands. If vengeance be demanded, let it come upon our enemies from the Lord, and not from us.

21. He who so far yields to passion as to let it get the mastery of him, is "overcome of evil." But we must conquer and overcome evil, by opposing to it the devout and self-contained temper which always looks to the Lord.

(CHAPTER XIII.)

1. Let every soul be subject unto the higher powers. For there is no power but of God: the powers that be are ordained of God.

The Apostle speaks of the Power of the Roman Empire; and enjoins submission thereto, because the Emperor bore the sword of temporal rule by the grant and appointment of God Himself. And yet the Roman Empire had crushed the whole world under its weight, and knew not, nor recognized, the True God.

All temporal power and authority proceed ultimately from the Most High, whatever be the form of Government. All constituted and lawful Rulers hold office by His Permission, and act as ordained by Him.

2. Whosoever therefore resisteth the power, resisteth the ordinance of God: and

Resistance to Government is resistance to God, when such factious opposition springs of pride, self-will, ambition, or groundless discontent. And

they that resist shall receive to themselves damnation.

destruction shall follow upon the rebellious. Therefore the Church prays: "From all sedition, privy conspiracy, and rebellion, Good Lord deliver us." For these are scourges to any people.

3. For rulers are not a terror to good works, but to the evil. Wilt thou then not be afraid of the power? do that which is good, and thou shalt have praise of the same:

Well might the Apostle speak as he does: for more than once he had owed his life to the Imperial power: he had, on several occasions, been snatched from death at the hands of his own mad and hot-headed countrymen, and borne away in safety behind a barrier of Roman shields and swords. (Acts xxi. 31, 32, 35; xxii. 24; xxiii. 26–30; xxvii. 31, 32.) This protection the Apostle owed simply to GOVERNMENT as such; not to any love or regard for him, since the Roman sword at last gave him his mortal blow; but to a Government which has its settled principles, and which protects all its subjects alike. The spirit of the Jewish nation was a purely anarchical one; their national individualism drove them to extravagance of passion when any question affecting their narrow sectional interests arose. But the Roman Empire was a Power in the earth; harsh, stern, heartless, but calm, equable, and reliable. This Power saved the Apostle's life; and under this Power, the Religion of Jesus Christ enjoyed a protection which it would not have found at the hands of any less able to enforce the true idea of Government.

4. For he is the minister of GOD to thee for good. But if thou do that which is evil, be afraid; for he beareth not the sword in vain: for he is the minister of GOD, a revenger to *execute* wrath upon him that doeth evil.

The Ruler holding and exercising his office according to Law, is in his sphere, as much the Minister of GOD, as is the Bishop presiding over his Diocese. It is his duty, at once to protect all in their right, and to execute wrath upon the rebellious and the evil. And his acts have the sanction of the Most High.

5. Wherefore *ye* must needs be subject, not only for wrath, but also for conscience' sake.
6. For for this cause pay ye tribute also: for they are GOD's minis-

5. A double reason is here assigned why all should be loyal citizens: 1st. for the fear of punishment on disloyalty and treason; but 2dly, and higher, for conscience' sake, and as a part of Christian duty.

ters, attending continually upon this very thing.

7. Render therefore to all their dues: tribute to whom tribute *is due;* custom to whom custom; fear to whom fear; honour to whom honour.

6. "Tribute:" (See S. Matthew xvii. 24–27; S. Mark xii. 14–17.)

The idea is, that we are required, by God's Law, not merely to honour and obey the Civil Authority, but readily and cheerfully to bear our part in the expenses of the State; for our Rulers are God's Ministers, appointed for the purposes previously mentioned, and attending to the fulfilment of those duties.

7. "Tribute:" taxes on person or estate.

"Custom:" taxes on goods or merchandise.

8. Owe no man any thing, but to love one another: for he that loveth another hath fulfilled the law.

The Apostle, having enumerated very many duties, both private and public, goes on thus: "In short, owe no man any thing;" *i. e.*, see that you punctually fulfil every thing that can fairly be demanded of you. "And yet," he adds, "there is one thing which none can ever count to be sufficiently and duly rendered, and in which we must all remain perpetual debtors; and that is, the duty of Christian Charity and Love." "For if God so loved men, they ought, in like proportion, to love one another." "For he that loveth his neighbour as himself, hath fulfilled the Law;" hath done all that could be demanded.

9. For this, Thou shalt not commit adultery, Thou shalt not kill, Thou shalt not steal, Thou shalt not bear false witness, Thou shalt not covet; and if *there be* any other commandment, it is briefly comprehended in this saying, namely, Thou shalt love thy neighbour as thyself.

10. Love worketh no ill to his neighbour: therefore love *is* the fulfilling of the law.

9. All that the Apostle has said, hitherto, is reducible to the one idea, that a man love his neighbour as himself. All duties to the State, to the family, to society, may be at last resolved into the great Law of Charity; the "New Commandment" given by the Lord Himself; the Precept of that Virtue which is greater than Faith or Hope, which is the crown of all the rest.

An affirmative is expressed by a negative. "Love works all good to his neighbour:" Love is the motive power to every kind of benefit and blessing; therefore Love is our part, the sum and substance of all that we have to do, the one principle in us which is better worth than the Righteousness of the Law; it is the very fulfilling of God's will.

11. And that, knowing the time, that now *it is* high time to awake out of sleep: for now *is* our salvation nearer than when we believed.

And these things should be borne in mind and meditated upon, and fully wrought out by us, while we have time. For the World grows old; and even already the ends of the world are upon us; and, to each believer, the critical moment, and the Awful Day, are nearer than they were when he first set forth on the journey. The swift passing away of Time, and the impending of Eternity, are reasons why men should arouse themselves from thoughtlessness and sloth, and be working while they have the time.

12. The night is far spent, the day is at hand: let us therefore cast off the works of darkness, and let us put on the armour of light.

13. Let us walk honestly, as in the day; not in rioting and drunkenness, not in chambering and wantonness, not in strife and envying.

14. But put ye on the Lord Jesus Christ, and make not provision for the flesh, to *fulfil* the lusts *thereof*.

12. "Ecce nox hujus vitæ præterit, vitaque properat ad finem; adest æternitatis dies semper duratura." The night of this present life, the day of the world to come: for this mortal state is but a night compared to that blessedness which shall be revealed when God shall be all in all. And again, as Theodoret remarks, the period before the Incarnation was the night of this world, when "the people sat in darkness;" but the time of ignorance is past; and now, since the Word hath been made Flesh, it is day, even the day of knowledge, and the rising of the Sun of Righteousness. Henceforth, men should live as new creatures.

13. Fleshly lusts, and mental pride, are two great downfalls for the soul. So, our first parents would be wise, and would gratify the appetite; and the end thereof was death.

14. To put on the Lord Jesus Christ, is to be like Him in mind, and to imitate Him in act; so that Christ shall visibly appear in us, as the garment in him who is clad therein. And the Apostle forbids all unnecessary study of the flesh, unto which it suffices that it live and be well, but for which no luxury should be allowed to minister indulgence.

(CHAPTER XIV.)

The Apostle treats, in this chapter, of things indifferent; not of matters of faith, nor of things of ecclesiastical regulation. For as respects the Faith, all compromises are sinful: and things indifferent in themselves, are rendered important and necessary, if regulated by the law of the Church of Christ; they cease, then, to be indifferent, and assume a character of relative obligation.

At that period, opposing systems met with a shock: the old died with a hard and bitter struggle, and the new rose above the ruins. Hence, the controversies in the earliest days.

The Jews, converted to Christianity, would have retained the Mosaic orders respecting meats and times; and they upbraided the Gentile converts for not observing the same: while the Gentiles sneered at the Jewish Christians for what they called, and correctly, a weakness. The Apostle meets both parties, and reproves each; exhorting them to observe Charity, and neither to despise nor revile one another.

1. Him that is weak in the faith receive ye, *but* not to doubtful disputations.

1. This is a general principle. The man who is yet weak and not fully instructed in the faith, should be kindly received, and, as it were, taken by the hand, and led along in a friendly spirit: not entertained with continual controversy respecting things doubtful and indifferent, nor vexed with disputings whether he be right or wrong in non-essential points.

2. For one believeth that he may eat all things: another, who is weak, eateth herbs.

2. The general principle is applied to a particular case. For example, one (the Gentile) believes that he may eat, of what he chooses; another (the Jew, brought up under a different system) would limit himself to herbs, if necessary, rather than partake of certain kinds of meat, or of meats prepared in a certain way.

3. Let not him that eateth despise him that eateth not; and let not him which eateth not judge him that eateth: for God hath received him.

3. There are faults to be avoided on each side: the Gentile must not despise the Jew for weakness, nor must the Jew accuse the Gentile of impiety. God hath received each alike, in the Catholic Church, and each has the same hope of salvation.

4. Who art thou that judgest another man's servant? to his own master he standeth or falleth. Yea, he shall be holden up: for GOD is able to make him stand.

4. Why, O Jew, dost thou thus arbitrarily judge the Gentile? He belongs to another: supposing him to be wrong, it is no affair of thine: his own Master shall judge him, even GOD. And the Gentile shall not be condemned: the same GOD who forbade meats under the Law, may permit their use under the Gospel.

5. One man esteemeth one day above another: another esteemeth every day *alike*. Let every man be fully persuaded in his own mind.

5. A second illustration of the principle first stated: men differ respecting the observance of certain days, commanded under the Law but not enjoined any longer. The Feasts of the Church, subsequently established by her authority, are not here intended; but the abrogated ordinances of the Mosaic Ritual. The Apostle says that brotherly concord should not be disturbed for those things; but that each man should pursue what course seemed to him best, since they were indifferent and non-essential.

6. He that regardeth the day, regardeth *it* unto the Lord; and he that regardeth not the day, to the Lord he doth not regard *it*. He that eateth, eateth to the Lord, for he giveth GOD thanks; and he that eateth not, to the Lord he eateth not, and giveth GOD thanks.

6. They, amongst whom these idle and unprofitable controversies might arise, were all Christians: it ought to be taken for granted, that each man, in whatsoever course he might adopt, meant to act reverently toward GOD: he that observed days, must be supposed to do so as intending thereby to honour the Lord; and he that declined to observe particular days, must be presumed to mean to hallow every day alike: so too in fasting, each must be acknowledging the same Lord as his Father and as the Provider of all his wants. This reflection should make both parties careful of judging, censuring, or condemning.

7. For none of us liveth to himself, and no man dieth to himself.
8. For whether we live, we live unto the Lord; and whether we die, we die unto the

Each must be thus charitably supposed to intend to honour GOD. For Christians are not their own. In life, in death, they are the Lord's. And they were bought by Christ, and are His. For these reasons, therefore, ought brotherly love to be kept, and

Lord: whether we live therefore, or die, we are the Lord's.

9. For to this end Christ both died, and rose, and revived, that he might be Lord both of the dead and living.

10. But why dost thou judge thy brother? or why dost thou set at nought thy brother? for we shall all stand before the judgment seat of Christ.

11. For it is written, *As* I live, saith the Lord, every knee shall bow to me, and every tongue shall confess to GOD.

12. So then every one of us shall give account of himself to GOD.

13. Let us not therefore judge one another any more: but judge this rather, that no man put a stumblingblock or an occasion to fall in *his* brother's way.

14. I know, and am persuaded by the Lord Jesus, that *there is* nothing unclean of itself: but to him that esteemeth any thing to be unclean, to him *it is* unclean.

the best construction put upon every one's actions and practices.

But again, there is another point of view, in which the custom of rash censuring and misrepresentation of motive appears especially indecent and wrong. They who thus judge, must themselves be judged (awful thought!) by Christ. Better to be preparing for one's own account, than to be curiously and uncharitably engaged about the faults of others.

In verse 13 there occurs the figure called Antanaclasis, or the repetition of the same word in a different sense. "Judge," first means "censure," or "condemn;" afterward it means, "consider and resolve." And here the Apostle lays down another general principle; that no one should use his liberty in things non-essential in such a way as to harm his brother, or endanger his salvation. Compare with this 1 Cor. viii. and x., where the same principle is applied to particular cases.

The Apostle, resuming the former illustration, speaks again of the Mosaic rules and orders concerning meats. No meats are unclean, absolutely: but they may become so relatively. For though it is a matter of entire indifference, in itself, what or how a man may eat: yet, through the accident of position, these things may become, to some man, of grave importance, and his salvation may seem to turn upon them. This possibility ought to be borne in mind, and the action should be shaped accordingly.

15. But if thy brother be grieved with *thy* meat, now walkest thou not charitably. Destroy not him with thy meat, for whom Christ died.

If, in respect to non-essentials, one so order himself as greatly to offend and scandalize a brother, he breaks the rule of Christian Charity: for that rule bids us not to grieve or pain or distress those for whom the Lord gave His

Blood. Such scandal and grief might have been produced, in those days, by eating before another what was abomination to him: it might be produced, in any day, by wantonly shocking another's feelings, or doing violence to his prejudices. All such acts are contrary to the spirit of the Gospel. See 1 Cor. x. 19–33.

16. Let not then your good be evil spoken of:
17. For the kingdom of God is not meat and drink; but righteousness, and peace, and joy in the Holy Ghost.
18. For he that in these things serveth Christ *is* acceptable to God, and approved of men.
19. Let us therefore follow after the things which make for peace, and things wherewith one may edify another.
20. For meat destroy not the work of God. All things indeed *are* pure; but *it is* evil for that man who eateth with offence.

Christians ought so to conduct themselves, as that the World may find no ground of charge and accusation against the religion which they profess: for our calling is not to useless formalities, but to the practice of divine and heavenly virtues in the Holy Ghost. And a religion, so lovely in its design and intention, ought not to be brought to public shame by idle contentions about things in which no principle is involved. Verses 18 and 19 need no comment.

20. The Apostle speaks very strongly: the danger would seem to be, that among the Jewish converts some were found, so wedded to the rules and precepts of their former mode of life, that they would rather renounce Christianity, than leave them off: he then who would persist in heaping contempt upon them, in those respects, might perhaps drive them to apostasy, and thus destroy the handiwork of God.

"All things are pure:" he had said this before, verse 14. Nevertheless, he sins, who uses food permitted to him, in such a way as to scandalize his brother.

21. *It is* good neither to eat flesh, nor to drink wine, nor *any thing* whereby thy brother stumbleth, or is offended, or is made weak.
22. Hast thou faith? have *it* to thyself before God. Happy *is* he that condemneth not himself in that thing which he alloweth.

21. It is, therefore, best to consult, 1st, the good of our neighbour, and 2dly, our own inclinations.

22. He addresses the stronger brethren. You have faith, clear, and firm; you know that all things are lawful: and you know, that the scruples of the weaker are foolish and baseless. Never mind: keep your convictions to yourself, and to God's Eye, nor parade offensively before the world your

strength of mind; let it suffice, that the Lord knoweth all. He is happy, indeed, who is not condemned by his conscience for mistaken action in respect to things about which his intellectual judgments were entirely correct.

23. And he that doubteth is damned if he eat, because *he eateth* not of faith: for whatsoever *is* not of faith is sin.

23. What the Apostle here says, respecting the special subject of meats, is really a principle of the highest importance and of the widest application. His words amount to this: that the Conscience of each must be the Guide: if a man hesitates, and doubts, and fluctuates between opinions respecting any thing which he would do, he is in great danger; and if thus doubtful, he eat, or drink, or indulge (in whatsoever particular the trial may occur), then is he guilty of sin; and he knows that he is, because he is condemned and judged by his conscience; for the conscience declared somewhat to be unlawful or inexpedient, which nevertheless he did; and thus is his condemnation sealed, since whatsoever is contrary to the dictates of conscience is certainly sin to him who does it, as it were, in the face and in the teeth of that monitor within.

Thus in this 14th chapter, have we three Rules respecting things indifferent:—

1st. That we contend not one with another in regard to them:

2dly. That we use our Christian liberty with constant reference to the welfare of our brethren:

3dly. That we walk by the Conscience in all things doubtful.

And, lastly, we should note that nothing which is here said can fairly be quoted by heretics as against the Rites and Ceremonies, the Rules and Requirements, of the Church System; because the Apostle is speaking of the things pertaining to the Mosaic Dispensation, which had passed away; and not, in anywise, of the Feasts, Fasts, &c., of the Church. These last are a part of Christ's gift to us in her; and among the things which she hath ordained, there can be nothing indifferent, to the faithful spirit and to the disciplined will.

(CHAPTER XV.)

1. We then that are
strong ought to bear the
infirmities of the weak,
and not to please our-
selves.

The subject treated in the preceding chapter is enlarged upon, with fresh arguments.

"Strong." The Gentiles especially are addressed, who were accustomed to despise the Jewish converts as weak. They are exhorted to consider others, and not themselves. "To bear," is, to bear with; to be indulgent toward.

2. Let every one of
us please *his* neighbour
for *his* good to edifica-
tion.

2. "For his good." It does not say, that a man should study to please his neighbour in *all* things, but only in those which are for his neighbour's good.

3. For even Christ
pleased not himself;
but, as it is written,
The reproaches of them
that reproached thee
fell on me.
4. For whatsoever
things were written
aforetime were written
for our learning, that we
through patience and
comfort of the scrip-
tures might have hope.

Christ is the example and rule. He lived not for Himself, but for us; He gave Himself for us. Therefore, we should live for each other, and yield one to another. For this is the lesson which the Scriptures were written to teach.

4. "Patience:" of which, in the Lord, and the Saints, the Scriptures give instances.

"Comfort:" for the Scriptures cheer and console in all trials.

"Hope:" namely, of eternal blessedness and rest.

5. Now the GOD of
patience and consola-
tion grant you to be
likeminded one toward
another according to
Christ Jesus:
6. That ye may with
one mind *and* one
mouth glorify GOD,
even the Father of our
Lord Jesus Christ.
7. Wherefore receive
ye one another, as
Christ also received us
to the glory of GOD.

5. All alike, Gentile and Jewish converts, are now addressed, and comprehended in a common benediction of unity and peace. And Christ is again proposed to all as an ensample: thus shall every thing redound to the Divine Glory:—let this, evermore, be the End; "*Ad majorem Dei gloriam.*"

8. Now I say that
Jesus Christ was a min-
ister of the circumcis-
ion for the truth of GOD,
to confirm the promises
made unto the fathers:
9. And that the Gen-

To Gentile and Jew alike, Christ speaketh: the Gentile must remember that the Lord came of the Hebrews, and was a Preacher, an Apostle, and an Evangelist of that nation first, that

tiles might glorify God for *his* mercy; as it is written, For this cause I will confess to thee among the Gentiles, and sing unto thy name.
10. And again he saith, Rejoice, ye Gentiles, with his people.
11. And again, Praise the Lord, all ye Gentiles; and laud him, all ye people.
12. And again, Esaias saith, There shall be a root of Jesse, and he that shall rise to reign over the Gentiles; in him shall the Gentiles trust.
13. Now the God of hope fill you with all joy and peace in believing, that ye may abound in hope, through the power of the Holy Ghost.
14. And I myself also am persuaded of you, my brethren, that ye also are full of goodness, filled with all knowledge, able also to admonish one another.
15. Nevertheless, brethren, I have written the more boldly unto you in some sort, as putting you in mind, because of the grace that is given to me of God,
16. That I should be the minister of Jesus Christ to the Gentiles, ministering the gospel of God, that the offering up of the Gentiles might be acceptable, being sanctified by the Holy Ghost.
17. I have therefore

He might show the truth of God and His promises as fulfilled (verse 8): while the Jews should recollect the prophecies concerning the Gentiles, and glorify God in that salvation which was announced to them of old (9–12). And so should all be filled with joy, in believing in the gradual but sure working out of the Eternal plans and purposes of the Almighty, (verse 13).

14. The Apostle apologizes for writing; it was not that he thought them ignorant or evil (see i. 8). He begins and ends with praises of that grand and renowned community, the Church at Rome. Compare with this, his quite different way of addressing the corrupt Corinthians, and the ignorant Galatians: (1 Cor. i. 11; iii. 3; vi. 1, 5, 7; &c., &c.; and Gal. i. 6; iii. 1.)

15. "The more boldly." Somewhat more freely than was necessary.

"Putting in mind:" not as if they were ignorant, but as reminding them of what they knew.

"Because, &c." As though irresistibly impelled by the spirit of his office.

16. For he was especially the Apostle to the Gentiles.

"Offering up." The language is Sacerdotal: the Ministry is a true Priesthood: to preach, to baptize, are, in their way, priestly functions: the

whereof I may glory through Jesus Christ in those things which pertain to God.

18. For I will not dare to speak of any of those things which Christ hath not wrought by me, to make the Gentiles obedient, by word and deed,

19. Through mighty signs and wonders, by the power of the Spirit of God; so that from Jerusalem, and round about unto Illyricum, I have fully preached the gospel of Christ.

20. Yea, so have I strived to preach the gospel, not where Christ was named, lest I should build upon another man's foundation:

21. But as it is written, To whom he was not spoken of, they shall see: and they that have not heard shall understand.

22. For which cause also I have been much hindered from coming to you.

23. But now having no more place in these parts, and having a great desire these many years to come unto you;

24. Whensoever I take my journey into Spain, I will come to you: for I trust to see you in my journey, and to be brought on my way thitherward by you, if first I be somewhat filled with your *company*.

conversion and salvation of souls is a perpetual oblation. Who shall venture to exercise these so high functions, except he be called of God, as was Aaron?

He intimates that his ministry had not been wanting in proofs of God's blessing upon it. But on the contrary, it had been abundantly crowned with favours and mercies, and with unusual signs and miraculous powers.

19. "Round about." Not by a direct way, but in a circuit, through the Oriental and Pontic regions.

20. This was the course which the Apostle seems to have marked out for himself; to strike always for unoccupied positions, and for fields where the Gospel was yet unknown. And thus (verse 21) he had fulfilled an ancient prophecy; making himself one instance among others, of its truth and applicability.

22. To wit, by the obligation to visit and preach in places whither the Gospel had not yet been carried: this had detained him.

23. The Apostle mentions his plans for the future: he designs a mission to Spain, and will visit Italy on his way thither.

25. But now I go unto Jerusalem to minister unto the saints.

26. For it hath pleased them of Macedonia and Achaia to make a certain contribution for the poor saints which are at Jerusalem.

27. It hath pleased them verily; and their debtors they are. For if the Gentiles have been made partakers of their spiritual things, their duty is also to minister unto them in carnal things.

25. The poverty of the Christians at Jerusalem was great: and S. Paul had been intrusted specially with the care of providing for their wants (Gal. ii. 10). For this purpose he was in the habit of making collections and receiving offerings for them wherever he went; and when these amounts became considerable, he would return, with what he had gathered, to Jerusalem. (See Acts xxiv. 17; 2 Cor. viii. 4; 2 Cor. ix. 1–5. &c., &c.)

28. When therefore I have performed this, and have sealed to them this fruit, I will come by you into Spain.

28. He proposes to set out for Spain, after he has taken to Jerusalem the amount of the offerings which he had then in his hands for them. "Sealed to them this fruit: *i. e.*, paid over to them in full that result of his labours and of the benevolence of the faithful.

29. And I am sure that, when I come unto you, I shall come in the fulness of the blessing of the gospel of Christ.

30. Now I beseech you, brethren, for the Lord Jesus Christ's sake, and for the love of the Spirit, that ye strive together with me in *your* prayers to God for me;

31. That I may be delivered from them that do not believe in Judæa; and that my service which *I have* for Jerusalem may be accepted of the saints;

32. That I may come unto you with joy by the will of God, and may with you be refreshed.

33. Now the God of peace *be* with you all. Amen.

29–33. The concluding verses of the chapter are so simple and clear, as to require no explanation. He evidently anticipates danger in visiting Jerusalem at that time: by the unbelieving Jews he was bitterly hated, and to the Jewish converts he was an object of suspicion: he trusts, therefore, to be delivered from the malice of his foes, and, by the proof of his zeal and love, to be rendered more acceptable to those doubtful brethren, who would not yet give him their confidence and affection.

(CHAPTER XVI.)

The Epistle closes with salutations to the Church at large, and to divers of the faithful who are specially mentioned by name. It needs but little comment, now; although this chapter forms a peaceful picture to which the mind will always gladly return, and on which it may love to dwell.

1. I commend unto you Phebe our sister, which is a servant of the church which is at Cenchrea:

2. That ye receive her in the Lord, as becometh saints, and that ye assist her in whatsoever business she hath need of you: for she hath been a succourer of many, and of myself also.

1. Phebe: a Deaconess of the church at Cenchrĕa, which is a seaport and suburb of Corinth, on the Saronic gulf: S. Paul was probably about to sail from that port on his way back to Jerusalem, and this Epistle was intrusted to her, to deliver it at Rome, whither she was journeying.

3. Greet Priscilla and Aquila my helpers in Christ Jesus:

4. Who have for my life laid down their own necks: unto whom not only I give thanks, but also all the churches of the Gentiles.

5. Likewise *greet* the church that is in their house. Salute my wellbeloved Epænetus, who is the first-fruits of Achaia unto Christ.

6. Greet Mary, who bestowed much labour on us.

7. Salute Andronicus and Junia, my kinsmen, and my fellowprisoners, who are of note among the apostles, who also were in Christ before me.

3. Priscilla is mentioned first, for she was converted before her husband; second in the order of nature, but first in the order of grace: so says one of the ancients. The well-known history of these two memorable persons is traced in the Acts and Apostolic Epistles. They had even risked their lives for Saint Paul.

5. Epænĕtus, one of the first converts to the faith, in Asia Minor: for the true reading is probably Asia: we are elsewhere told that the house of Stephanas was the first-fruits of Achaia (1 Cor. xvi. 15).

6. It has been inferred that Andronīcus and Junia were Apostles: it is not however certain that this was the case, as the words do not require that sense.

8. Greet Amplias my beloved in the Lord.

9. Salute Urbane, our helper in Christ, and Stachys my beloved.

10. Salute Apelles approved in Christ. Salute them which are of Aristobulus' *houshold.*

11. Salute Herodion my kinsman. Greet them that be of the *houshold* of Narcissus, which are in the Lord.

12. Salute Tryphena and Tryphosa, who labour in the Lord. Salute the beloved Persis, which laboured much in the Lord.

13. Salute Rufus chosen in the Lord, and his mother and mine.

14. Salute Asyncritus, Phlegon, Hermas, Patrobas, Hermes, and the brethren which are with them.

15. Salute Philologus, and Julia, Nereus, and his sister, and Olympas, and all the saints which are with them.

16. Salute one another with an holy kiss. The churches of Christ salute you.

17. Now I beseech you, brethren, mark them which cause divisions and offences contrary to the doctrine which ye have learned; and avoid them.

18. For they that are such serve not our Lord Jesus Christ, but their own belly; and by good words and fair speeches deceive the hearts of the simple.

19. For your obedience is come abroad unto all *men.* I am glad therefore on your behalf: but yet I would have you wise unto that which is good, and simple concerning evil.

20. And the GOD of peace shall bruise Satan under your feet shortly. The grace of our Lord Jesus Christ *be* with you. Amen.

17. He warns them against the arts of certain schismatics, who had appeared among them and infested them, or who might probably be plying their evil arts there as elsewhere before.

18. This warning is supported by two sufficient causes for its being given; 1st, because the persons in question were vile and contemptible in character, and selfish in their motives: and,

19. 2dly. Because the faith of the Roman Church was a common treasure of the whole Christian body, and any failure on their part would work wide mischief.

20. The Apostle lastly assures them of GOD's aid, and predicts their final triumph over all the powers of darkness.

21. Timotheus my workfellow, and Lucius, and Jason, and Sosipater, my kinsmen, salute you.

22. I Tertius, who wrote *this* epistle, salute you in the Lord.

23. Gaius mine host, and of the whole church, saluteth you. Erastus the chamberlain of the city saluteth you, and Quartus a brother.

24. The grace of our Lord Jesus Christ *be* with you all. Amen.

Others also salute the Roman Christians, through the Apostle, who mentions them by name: among these is Tertius, an amanuensis, who copied out the letter, or wrote it at S. Paul's dictation.

And then, finally, not without reference to that great scheme of salvation, which he has before mentioned, and which he seems to have ever in mind, the Apostle brings this Epistle to a close, commending them once more to God, and ascribing to Him all praise and glory.

25. Now to him that is of power to stablish you according to my gospel, and the preaching of Jesus Christ, according to the revelation of the mystery, which was kept secret since the world began,

26. But now is made manifest, and by the scriptures of the prophets, according to the commandment of the everlasting God, made known to all nations for the obedience of faith:

27. To God only wise, *be* glory through Jesus Christ for ever. Amen.

¶ Written to the Romans from Corinthus, *and sent* by Phebe servant of the church at Cenchrea.

7*

Lord Jesus Christ,

RAISE US FROM THE DEATH OF SIN, THAT WE MAY WALK IN NEWNESS OF LIFE;

MAY THY DEATH EXTINGUISH IN US THE OLD ADAM;

MAY THY RISING AGAIN CALL BACK OUR INNER MAN TO LIFE;

MAY THY BLOOD WASH US FROM SIN;

MAY THY RESURRECTION CLOTHE US WITH THE GARMENT OF RIGHTEOUSNESS:

To Thee, O True Life,

DO WE, DEAD IN SINS, LIFT UP OUR EYES AFAR OFF:

To Thee, O True Righteousness,

DO WE, NAKED AND IN MISERY, TURN US FOR THE CLOTHING OF THY SPIRIT:

To Thee, O True Salvation,

DO WE, CONDEMNED FOR SIN, BETAKE US FOR REFUGE:

THOU ONLY ART WORTHY,

O Lamb that wast Slain,

TO RECEIVE MIGHT, RICHES, GLORY, AND DOMINION,

SEEING THAT THOU ART, TO ALL,

THE WAY, THE TRUTH, AND THE LIFE.

www.ingramcontent.com/pod-product-compliance
Lightning Source LLC
LaVergne TN
LVHW011230110826
845150LV00006B/1593

* 9 7 8 1 4 2 5 5 1 4 6 3 1 *